The Commandments of Womanhood

Emiko Love

The Commandments of Womanhood

The Commandments of Womanhood

Table of Contents

DEDICATION	5
PREFACE	7
LOVE THYSELF	13
PROTECT THY ENERGY	49
RULE THY OWN HAPPINESS	54
YOUR BODY IS A TEMPLE: ACT LIKE IT	111
SEEK NO VALIDATION	126
THOU SHALL NOT SETTLE FOR INCONSISTENCY	132
YOUR PAST SHALL NOT DEFINE YOUR FUTURE	141
FINANCE THYSELF WITH A WEALTHY MIND	147
BECOME THY IDEAL MATE	158
ALWAYS REMEMBER THY ROYALTY	166
EPILOGUE	177

The Commandments of Womanhood

The Commandments of Womanhood

Dedication

This book is dedicated to all the lost Queens who have tipped their crowns, and the others who have not yet discovered their Royalty. Never let your past define your future, for everyday begins a new chapter, and the past is but a distant memory.

In loving memory of Yolanda and Larry McDowell

The Commandments of Womanhood

The Commandments of Womanhood

Preface

Throughout my life I've had the pleasure of having so many different conversations with women, and during those conversations my heart shattered as I heard their journey into womanhood. No matter the background or age bracket, one thing remained the same: We are all in one way hurting, or have been hurt, in our journey to womanhood. That pain has ultimately shaped us into the type of people we've become. I'd often joke with my friends on how women needed their own bible or handbook that helps guide them through life. Deep down I knew there was more truth to those words than humor, simply because it has always been something we so desperately needed to shift the mindset of our generation.

There are so many acts of violence we commit against ourselves that we are not even aware of, so many ways in which we are being taken advantage of mentally, physically, and emotionally. Living in a world where

The Commandments of Womanhood

we'd rather expose our bodies than expose our minds because we've been brainwashed into thinking that is the only way to reach ultimate success. We'd rather shame our sister than let her know how beautiful, loved, appreciated, and important she is. Somewhere along the way we stopped being guided by our mothers and the women around us. It has become painfully evident that we've lost sight of who we are.

    We have so much power within us, but we often lose sight of that because we've been broken. Mainstream media has made it okay for us not to love ourselves; and our damaged hearts are somehow left on display to be applauded for likes and views. There haven't been many positive representations of women in several years within mainstream media; and the ones who are doing something positive don't get nearly as much recognition as they deserve because their accomplishments are often dimmed by the mundane distractions of our society. The fake woke come and go, but in actuality there are not many who truly advocate for us without seeking personal gain.

The Commandments of Womanhood

It seems as though our value is now somehow determined on the amount of plastic surgery and enhancements we've gotten in order to make us acceptable within society's standard of beauty. I'll admit, being exposed to this has even made me consider going under the knife a few times because it's so easy to get misguided by a false sense of beauty and reality. I quickly shake away the idea each time, but the thoughts still haunt my subconscious and linger in the back of my mind. It almost seems taboo, or rare, to be bare-faced and love the skin you are in. We make ourselves so accessible to judgement, but have never been taught to have strong enough mindsets to withstand harsh criticism.

As women we have to stop placing our own deep-rooted insecurities and fears onto the people around us. Feminism is about believing that all women matter—not just the ones who are physically appealing in the eyes of mainstream media. You cannot simply say you uplift women when you constantly bash the closest women around you. How dare we bash and ridicule a fellow fallen Queen instead of trying to raise her up? We often

The Commandments of Womanhood

result to making drastic changes to our outer beings not knowing that our inner beauty shines beyond our exterior. As women, we are so afraid of becoming aware and taking responsibility for everything that has come into our lives. So many mothers don't love themselves and pass that same self-hatred down to their offspring, oblivious to the cycle that they are beginning.

When I first began writing this book I didn't know what this would become. Maybe this would be another project I got so passionate about and eventually let collect dust in the corner. However, once I began writing I couldn't stop. The more negative images of women I was surrounded with, the clearer it became that this book was bigger than me and my procrastination. This is a reminder of the greatness we've forgotten. I actually wrote this within a two-week time span only to leave it untouched for almost a year. Something as simple as a small handbook evolved into something bigger than I'd even imagined.

It is extremely important to remind ourselves of the Queens we are, and how important it is to remember our royalty. So many of us don't know how to love

The Commandments of Womanhood

ourselves and protect our energy, let alone take care of finances. This guide is the very thing we should keep in our back pockets to remind us how great we are and inspire us to press on regardless of what comes our way. I hope you find healing within these passages and comfort within the stories I share. I was apprehensive about being so transparent, but I think this is necessary. We came into this world as Queens, and Queens we shall forever remain.

The Commandments of Womanhood

The Commandments of Womanhood

Love Thyself

"Hey beautiful, do you know you are a Queen?"

Some can define self-love as the regard of one's wellbeing and happiness, but I believe a woman's love for herself is by far more profound. The journey is one that is endless and the love a woman has for herself should bloom as prodigious as the most beautiful flower at its peak in full bloom. Loving yourself in a world that glorifies self-destruction and hate is a hard thing to do. Self-love is extremely important with women, for we are the givers of life and birth the nation.

By having such a big responsibility in society, it is extremely crucial that we be mindful of the generational curses that have a habit of getting passed down to our offspring. It is our duty to break the cycles of self-hate that hold us captive. Social media has created an illusion of unrealistic beauty standards that don't

The Commandments of Womanhood

exist. So many women hide their insecurities behind a makeup brush, waist trainer, filter, or plastic surgery.

There is nothing wrong with beauty enhancements, but always remember you can only cover up a hole for so long; and unless it's properly patched up and corrected, a hole it shall remain. If you don't like something about your appearance, before changing it drastically, try finding the beauty within it and learning to love it. For many, this is a very difficult task because loving yourself is an everyday journey that never ends. We often ask ourselves: How can we love ourselves when we've never even been shown love properly to begin with? Many of us have been taught our first lessons of love by how our mothers treat us and how our fathers respect our mothers. For many the second one is never shown at all.

We tend to search for love in people and things before gaining it within. We'd rather substitute our pain for temporary gratification and then wonder why we are so broken—failing to realize that we haven't even bothered trying to make ourselves whole. Self-love begins with tricking the mind and conditioning the heart.

The Commandments of Womanhood

I've come in contact with so many beautiful women who tend to be insecure about the very things that make them extraordinary. So many times we let the people we love and care about diminish our self-worth. Giving another person that type of power would never be an option if we were fully secure in everything that makes us wonderful.

Always remember that there is perfection in the midst of imperfection. There is no such thing as a perfect woman because being imperfectly perfect is the greatest gift of all. I often wish that I lived in a filter-less generation. Not only do we hide behind filters on images, but also somehow we've stopped being unapologetically real. It's easier to conform when everybody accepts you than stand out when most are against you. It seems like so many people are afraid to just be themselves, not the made up versions of themselves that they pretend to be to seem cool, but the unapologetically unfiltered person that they truly are.

We live in a generation where women would rather celebrate their fake friends than appreciate their real friendships. They've stopped being true to who they are. The main reason being is because we stopped loving

The Commandments of Womanhood

ourselves. If you don't accept the real you, how can you celebrate the genuine people who come into your path? I can speak from experience that I've sabotaged a friendship or two in the past when I wasn't in the proper space to open up to new people.

As women, we tend to display our insecurities in one of two ways: the first being the obvious, hiding behind objects that mask the flaws that we aren't that proud of, and second, bringing others down for the fear that our most guarded insecurities may manifest within ourselves. Self-love begins with the mind. With that being said, protect your mind from things that can expose your hidden insecurities. When conditioning your mind, you must detox it of the negativity that nourishes your insecurities.

Take a step back from music that provides hatred, for you are opening yourself up to distractions that can secretly make their way into your mind. Have you ever listened to a song about heartbreak? While it may not even relate directly to you, sometimes you find yourself lost in the words feeling a way as well as subconsciously relating it to a situation that it probably has nothing to do

The Commandments of Womanhood

with. Your mind begins racing and you start to pick at things about yourself that you possibly could've done differently. You desperately try to find logic within what has caused a situation instead of accepting the lesson and moving forward. We've all done it at one time or another. I've done it, smacked myself for doing it, and the repeated the process again until I became aware of my pattern. Be careful of the things that you feed to your mind because it's more powerful than you know.

    Recently, I found myself having to stop listening to music by an artist I really enjoy for the simple fact that every song he makes degrades women. I never understood how men with daughters can create the most disrespectful music towards women and then wonder why their daughters self-sabotage themselves. So many men wonder how there can be so many broken women in the world when many times they've been the ones to contribute to it. Many of our first loves were our fathers, so how can we possibly feel like anyone will ever treat us with respect when our father figures don't respect women?

The Commandments of Womanhood

Let me let you in on a little secret that will be forever true and never change You are worthy. You are worthy of love, peace, happiness, and abundance. When learning to love yourself beyond your entire being, try to stay away from music, images, and ideas that have a way of fueling the insecurities you are trying to change into appreciations. We get so wrapped up in what is going on in the outside that world we forget to tune into ourselves completely. More importantly than that, we forget to tune into God.

While the internet has become a great source of information, it has ultimately become the source of our destruction. It has become a place where the broken and insecure hide to bring others down. So many times we find ourselves peeking at another's journey rather than evolving in our own. How many times have you been having a great time and stopped yourself from fully enjoying just to post on social media? We fail to realize that we no longer know how to have genuine fun and with doing that, another person is looking at the illusion that we choose to display only to begin feeling as though they are inadequate. We all look at each other's lives

The Commandments of Womanhood

unaware that the things we are seeing are simply smoke and mirrors. Everything around us in this day and age is an illusion that is sometimes unattainable. There are so many broken people that appear to have everything, and are secretly unhappy. Meanwhile, here you are possibly wishing you had their life when they're wishing they had your peace and contentment. Instead of tuning into the outside world, read, listen, and watch things that enhance your mind with positivity and nourish your heart.

My self-love journey has been a long, troubling road. Growing up I was so sure of myself, or at least for a while I thought I was. I grew up in a two parent household, until my dad passed away when I was about 8; and I had mother who loved me beyond measure, whom I lost right upon the cusp of me coming into my womanhood at 15. I grew up surrounded by widows and independent married women, but somehow I still managed to get lost in the sauce.

Throughout the majority of my adolescent years I was so convinced of who I was and then in the blink of an eye life happened. I had to figure out so many difficult lessons that I'd never been taught along the way

The Commandments of Womanhood

by simple trial and error. Years later I found myself looking up at 22, a broken young woman who didn't have the slightest clue about what it meant to truly love myself. Not having that motherly figure that I could truly trust with my delicate mind from 15 and on played a major role in the decisions I made. In a sense, I became my own mother and policed my own thoughts and emotions. It always seemed like the moment I found those motherly qualities in someone they'd either abandon me or turn their backs on me.

      As a teen I didn't date. I was always the cool home girl that everyone thought was confident and beautiful—but I had never dated. I wasn't single because I never liked anyone, but because the few times that I had put myself out there the feelings were never mutual, so I became detached. My pride never allowed me to want to deal with rejection. For a young woman as sure of herself as I thought I was, it was okay for a while; but as you get older and see more of your friends getting into serious relationships, you start to wonder why. Well, what is wrong with me? Am I really as beautiful as I've convinced myself? Did others feed me lies to boost a false sense of confidence? Why doesn't anyone I love or care about stay? What am I doing wrong and why doesn't it work out for me?

Subconsciously, I began to let those questions consume my thoughts until they got so loud I lost sight of the little girl who was shown love and reminded of her beauty daily. I met life and let me tell you it was freaking tough! I had a Cinderella type fantasy and an old school upbringing that convinced me that a man had to find me, so I didn't look. While this was a great way of thinking, I misconstrued that true love would somehow equate to my happily ever after. Always placing my happiness in the future instead of enjoying the present nearly tainted me.

Instead of elevating and becoming a better me, I became busy and buried the pain that I carried. I threw myself into school, got good grades, did the college thing for a while, started several businesses, got tripped by reality, started working for others(companies), got shoved by reality, became guarded, got kicked again by reality, obtained my independence, nearly got choked by reality, and then woke up 22 years broken. The irony of

The Commandments of Womanhood

it all was that I was convinced my first book would be a sarcastic humorous memoir called *22 Years a Virgin*; and here I am, a few weeks' shy of 24, slowly piecing myself together, writing a book to help piece other lost souls like myself together again.

The only love I'd known had been snatched away at the early age of 7, and every year that followed I found myself losing more people to the angel of death. Honestly, you would've thought I grew up at Inglewood Cemetery Mortuary as much as I watched my mother either plan or help plan a funeral. By 10 I could probably counsel you on grief as well as how to plan a funeral. I saw my mother hold it together so I suppressed my pain because her strength never allowed her to acknowledge hers. Now looking back, I realize the self-assured version of myself that I was convinced existed was just a figment of my imagination. I was lost, but so busy that I didn't know the self-love I was missing until I finally found it after all these years.

So many times we tell ourselves that we love the person we are when we don't. We lie to ourselves constantly to feel as if we have everything figured out. If

The Commandments of Womanhood

we can't even be honest with ourselves who can we be real with? I used to self-medicate with a sharp razor blade against my wrist, careful not to cut too deep and only deep enough so that my pain would ease. I had been nearly drowned at the age of 8 while at summer day camp by an older boy that used to feel up my underdeveloped breast, or as my best friend liked to call them at that age "baby fat" since I was on the chubby side. I never knew why I was afraid of guys for so long until I started to acknowledge what had me so fearful of surpassing my shyness and leading me to avoiding intimate affection all together.

As a teen I had plenty of guy friends, but I found comfort in being the "bro" and little sister to them. Guys had always tried to talk to me, but I'd always been too shy and scared of rejection to even acknowledge their advances. I had to lose myself completely to find myself beneath the battered soul that wasn't whole.

While working at a call center, my friend introduced me to online dating around 21 and I decided to give it a try. I didn't have my first real kiss until I was 21 and in my generation I honestly think that's unheard

The Commandments of Womanhood

of especially because all my friends had been kissing so early in life, way before training bras and tampons. It was my first date and to this day I don't think I told anyone that I paid for the movie. I was tired of waiting for the prince charming, so I convinced myself he didn't exist for me. I decided to kiss a couple of toads while waiting for him—if he ever did decide to show up.

He was a Puerto Rican and Cuban guy from New York who recently moved to LA. We'd been talking for a couple of months and I was finally comfortable enough to meet up with *him* because I like to feel people out before hanging out. He asked me out to the movies on Valentine's Day and I'd never had a real Valentine so I was excited. Here was this very attractive guy who was the epitome of what I thought was my type, looks-wise at least, who wanted to take me out. In all actuality I was taking myself out, but I convinced myself otherwise.

The day of our date he mentioned that he was running short on cash because he had to pay rent so I decided to treat since I didn't want to reschedule especially since I made it a habit to try and put myself out there more. After we went to the movies, we walked

The Commandments of Womanhood

around downtown Los Angeles for what seemed like hours; first quiet then gradually talking.

He reminded me a lot of my high school male best friend and crush- the only difference is he didn't play the game of leading me on only to let me fall alone. This guy actually seemed interested in me the same way I was with him. I had brought some shots with me and we tossed them back at a park near Persian Square. It got quiet and my heart began racing while my mind was having an argument about if he was really even attracted to me since he hadn't made a move yet.

Through texts and video chats he seemed very into me, but now I was just a ball of confusion. The main reason is I didn't want to be over 21 without my first real kiss. Suddenly, mid-thought, it happened: he wrapped his arms around me as we sat on a bench staring into the night sky and he kissed me.

Now, before you guys start letting your minds get carried away thinking this is a picture perfect movie scene, I'm going to stop you right there. This was definitely no fairy tale and I did not see any fireworks in this moment. He was very aggressive, had way too much tongue, and his mouth tasted like cigarettes mixed with hints of funk. I was repulsed to say the least. For a split second I nearly questioned my sexuality because here I was sitting in a park kissing this fine guy on Valentine's Day and I was utterly repulsed. As I allowed him feel me up and kiss me I began to feel like that little girl at day camp who couldn't fight my attacker back, but this time it was my newfound insecurities that were holding me captive. While letting his hands travel freely with no hesitation, I allowed him to kiss me while feeling violated and disgusted. We hung out once more after that night, but I let that fling eventually die down because what he was after I just was not ready give out—especially to him.

  Now we move on to 22 and I was still a virgin. I had never kissed a guy that I actually enjoyed kissing and it seemed like everyone around me was having all this wild magical sex. Eventually, I deleted my dating profile after the first guy only to find myself on a new site when I met *him,* "The Artist" or as I'd like to call him "Houdini". He had more disappearing acts than a magician, but let me not jump ahead of myself. It didn't

The Commandments of Womanhood

start off that way, but I will tell you this, there were probably a million and one signs that yelled "Girl, leave this man alone!"

He was about four years older than me and we had actually started talking a little before I turned 22. A college educated man with what seemed like real goals and he wasn't just into talking about sex. He was so sweet and our conversations flowed effortlessly. *The Artist* had the ability to make me feel so comfortable and I told him things that I hadn't even told my closest friends at the time. We'd text and chat all day about any and everything. I thought he was perfect and then he dropped a bomb on me.

He knew I was very inexperienced and somehow we ended up on a conversation about what we were into and what I thought I was into sexually. He then proceeded to tell me that he had dabbled from time to time in the past. I was so confused and naive as to what he meant by this. I began to probe with more investigative questions because I refused to believe that the first guy that I felt like I had a real connection with was into anything too bizarre. He proceeds to tell me that he'd messed with a couple of trans-women before on a few occasions, but he usually stuck to watching the porn because it was safer. In my mind I was so taken aback because just a few weeks' prior a coworker of mine found out her man was cheating on her with trans-prostitutes and she blew a fuse. Was this what men were into these days? I never dated before so this was so new to me and beyond baffling.

  I began to ask more questions like if he knew beforehand or was it with ones that had undergone sex changes. My mind was blown when he admitted he was aware beforehand and that he'd never been with one who had a sex change. *The Artist* then goes on to tell me how he'd even given oral to one and enjoyed it. Devastated wasn't even the word for how I felt. We were getting ready to finally meet in person and he dropped the weirdest bomb on me. The crazy thing is he didn't even think he was gay or bisexual. He considered himself to be straight man that loved women.

  I told him I didn't think I could be with someone who was into that because I didn't want to put myself at risk especially if there could be a possibility that he could never be fully satisfied with me. He tried to turn my concerns into insecurities, so opened up to some friends about what happened. They thought it was disgusting and told me that I was right by ending things. First, I want to let you know that I have nothing against guys who are into transgender women, but I am sharing this story about how I found self-love and I can't leave anything that contributed to this out. This story is not to bash men who are gay, queer, or bisexual, but to shed light on how I settled for what I knew I didn't want because of feeling inadequate and unworthy.

So many of us settle for qualities in men we aren't comfortable with and we try to convince ourselves that we are okay with it because we don't trust in the Lord's promise. We often settle for what is around instead of believing that God will bring us what our hearts truly desire. Even if the guy hasn't engaged in homosexual activity, it could be other things such as him not valuing our love.

There are actually more women that don't come forward who know of their significant other's alternative lifestyle than the ones who actually speak up. This

The Commandments of Womanhood

happens so much that the ones who actually do are left feeling weird and alone. You are not weird or alone. There are many of us who have comprised our personal big no-no's before, in some way or another, whether we like to admit it or not. It might not even be as extreme as I've mentioned, but it happens. Our partner could be disrespectful or simply use us, and somehow our insecurities have taught us to turn the other cheek. Most of us accept a lot because we think it's as good as it gets, forgetting how precious we are. Never compromise your standards or morals for the fear of being alone, because it's not worth it. If you end up compromising yourself like I've done in the past, learn how to forgive yourself and set a better standard as to not repeat the action.

    I've had too many conversations with friends that have made excuses for the men that they love simply because they thought better wasn't out there for them. The fact is some of us are afraid of ending up alone. Some of us chase after the family man or the strong man because we grow up in broken homes. The average household in this day and age is broken, and we as women have a habit of chasing what we are missing with

The Commandments of Womanhood

hopes that it'll right the wrongs of our parents. We try so hard to create a different outcome for ourselves, but fail to deal with our pain first. I've never been dependent on defining myself within a relationship, but I've compromised myself in the past just for temporary affection at night.

    A few weeks went by and I didn't have anyone serious in rotation. I only went to work and back home, so I was convinced that I would never find anyone to help pass the time. When you're always to yourself like I was, it's easy to find comfort in a fun buddy. Why in the world didn't I stick with my first mind? I'll tell you why. I saw most of my closest friends and everybody around me in serious relationships. I couldn't help, but constantly feel like I was missing out on something because I'd never been in love or even maintained interest in anybody long enough to want to start a relationship with them. Against my better judgment, I texted him and let him know that I only said what I thought I should say because of my Christian upbringing. To be quite honest, I didn't want a man who wasn't

The Commandments of Womanhood

totally into women and I kicked myself everyday while entertaining him.

I let him know that I didn't judge him; but secretly, the only one I was really judging was myself because I didn't think I could do better. He was attractive and I felt like he was as good as it was going to get for me. What a shame it was to lose confidence in the wonderful person God has created me to be. In my mind, if someone was out there for me why hadn't I met him? The answer that I now know is because I did not yet know my purpose, I didn't know the extent of my worth, I wasn't trusting God to bring me my husband, and I definitely did not love myself like I thought I did. The night we began talking again he told me that my open mind made me so much more beautiful. I never had a man call me beautiful besides my family and my dad so sue me if that made me blush. Looking back, I now see those 22 years alone without companionship and love only made my self-esteem begin to dwindle.

We eventually met and he was the first guy that I let come over to my apartment. He began giving me a quick art lesson and somehow we began kissing. This time it was different. I actually enjoyed it and I said a silent prayer of relief for the fact that I was really into guys because I almost thought something was wrong with me and that I didn't like any gender. Our kisses got heavy, but he told me that we should wait. He said that my first time should be special and tried to begin filling my head with fairytales of a future that I knew would never happen.

At that point, I had given up the thought of falling in love and finding someone special. No matter how nice he and his kisses were, I decided not to allow myself to like him because I knew I'd only get hurt with the type of things that he was into. I met a few more guys offline and they all said the same thing: "You're a good girl and you should wait." Meanwhile, my friends were saying: "Girl, get out there." Putting myself out there was so difficult because I stayed to myself so much. If what the guys said were true, then why didn't they want me? Why didn't anyone want the virgin if she was so special? I wanted to lose my virginity on my own terms, not because I wanted to wait till marriage like my mother had at 32. At the rate I was going I feared I'd probably be older than her by the time I lost my virginity. Being suicidal during this time also contributed to me wanting to get it over with before I finally got the nerve to go out the way I wanted.

It seemed like when guys were coming to me for sex prior, I wasn't interested or trying to have it. I shut them down left and right with no hesitation. The irony is as I got older, in my Samantha Jones *Sex in the City* mentality, I couldn't get anyone to take my virginity even if I tried. Well, I wasn't trying that hard, but I was hopeful with the guys I did talk to. It was like guys were into me up until I answered the magic question and after the first date they'd never call again. *The Artist* stuck around, but I felt like he was pretending to fall harder than he was. My pride wouldn't let me be into him like he was into me even though I did find comfort in his companionship. He tried to talk about kids and all types of things to the point that I was actually scared he'd try to get me pregnant on purpose because the kid talk came so suddenly. He never had condoms; and after he told me what he was into, he'd be crazy to ever think I'd not use protection with him.

The Commandments of Womanhood

One time I got to a point where I didn't even care if it was him who took my virginity because at least we had sexual attraction and I trusted him in some aspects because he was honest for the most part. The funny thing is that all of our attempts just didn't happen, as if God were trying to warn me. This frustrated me to no end, and at times I felt like cursing God because I wanted the sin so desperately. Now, looking back, I'm lucky He didn't strike me down right then and there. The crazy things we do to sin and justify our sin is baffling.

To this day I don't even know this girl that I somehow morphed into. Becoming reckless, I didn't care about myself; and although I looked beautiful on the outside, I didn't feel that way. Between 15 and 22, I thought about suicide on a daily basis. Sometimes I'd purposely walk through dangerous neighborhoods late at night hoping that a stray bullet would somehow find its way to me. I wasn't really doing photography as much as usual since I got a job and no longer worked for myself. My clothing line that I started, after so much initial support, eventually dwindled down as well. There seemed to be no time to focus on any of my dreams or aspirations. Like most people, I just started working to survive.

I was working full time, and staying in an apartment that was more expensive than the money I was making at the time—I lost sight of my dreams and who I wanted to become. There was a period when I had to get a second job and I'd literally not even sleep most days because I got home so late from my second job. I hated my life and I felt so alone. The family I did have left didn't really come around or reach out to me. The close family friends that my mom had didn't even make a real effort to be in my life, and I got tired of reaching out to people who didn't reach out to me.

At almost 22, I was up to my neck in bills and I literally had no one I was comfortable enough to call to help me, not even God. To be so prideful not to even share your problems with God is suicide in itself. Figuring things out was all I knew how to do. I mainly got the job at the restaurant to eat because it was exhausting going to work 40 plus hours a week on little to no sleep and no food. This struggle eventually led me to taking out 4 payday loans to makes sure I paid my rent

The Commandments of Womanhood

on time. My cousin whom I considered an older brother even seemed like he disappeared when I needed him the most. Everybody had their own problems and that's why the few people I counted on couldn't help me during this time, which I realize now. The Payless slip resistant shoes that I wore to work literally had me with bruises and cuts on the bottom of my feet. I began to wonder how I hit rock bottom and why I got to this point.

On my 22nd birthday, I went to work intoxicated by alcohol and slept the whole day while my supervisor turned my phone off so I wouldn't have to take calls. I could finally fit into a jumpsuit I'd bought a year prior and it wasn't because of a good diet, but starvation. Eventually I did get a better job, but by then the damage was already done and I still wasn't fulfilled working for others when I knew I wanted more for my life. The craving for purpose makes you feel like your floating in limbo.

After getting my new job, I started being free, going out and drinking with my close friend at the time. She was a cute Asian girl that went to high school with my best friend. We'd often go different places and she'd

The Commandments of Womanhood

randomly hook up with different guys we'd meet. I remember being at a recording studio one time seeing a producer cut up and snort coke in front of me like it was just a normal thing to do. As he sniffed multiple white lines, I stared in pure bewilderment that this really happens outside of the movies. I'd never been much of a heavy partier and this wasn't something I was used to. Moments later my friend at the time went to a car with a guy we'd just met and gave him oral while I stayed in the studio with the coked out producer anticipating her return so we could leave. After that night I somehow knew I had to reevaluate the company I kept because in the 22 years I'd been living, I'd never been exposed to hardcore drugs like cocaine. I became conscious of what I was exposing myself to, but I still wasn't fully loving and valuing myself.

    After months of soul searching and various experiences, I decided I had to get to the bottom of what was holding me back—the first step being to love myself completely. I thought I began loving myself in the past with being comfortable within my weight, but I had to look deeper at my actions and realize I deserved more

The Commandments of Womanhood

than what I was giving to myself. The way I was portraying myself with the guys I became involved with was an indication of that. I put up with so many things I wasn't comfortable simply because I lost hope in finding a soul, so I settled for distant lovers.

Ultimately there had to become a point when I forgave myself for the things I was doing to myself. *The Artist* and me talked for around 3 years on and off. I could sit and pick at everything he did like being inconsistent and flakey, but I came to realize he wasn't the problem. I ultimately allowed him to continue his behavior and convinced myself that he was just something to keep me company in the meantime—I was the problem. What I have come to realize after so much self-reflection is he was ultimately the manifestation of all of my fears and insecurities.

Each time he disappeared or proved to be undependable, my heart mourned. My heart mourned not because I had deep feelings for him, but because I allowed a repeated cycle of loss that I experienced since I was young to continue. I was sabotaging myself emotionally while hardening my heart. Subconsciously, I

The Commandments of Womanhood

allowed myself to mourn in anger. Reality began to set in that I didn't need closure from him because pursuing that always lead to a temporary reconciliation. I had to forgive myself for compromising myself with men and not just with him, but the ones I dealt with before as well. *The Artist* was a manifestation of the hidden insecurities that I didn't like about myself from porn addiction to constantly isolating myself. I got mad at him for the things that I was doing to others, which was hypocritical of me. Although I wasn't flakey on his extreme level, I always closed myself off from people who simply just wanted to be there for me. During this time, I allowed myself to entertain a man who didn't match my ambition, nor value and care for me the way I should be valued and cared for, because it was my excuse to guard myself.

In the back of mind, I always knew this *situationship* wouldn't go anywhere despite the many times he said he wanted to build with me. Nevertheless, he was always there no matter how many times I cut him off for his inconsistency. He was my safety net. Women are very intuitive, and at most times we are very much

The Commandments of Womanhood

aware of when things or people aren't good for us; but we continue our habits anyway, out of comfort, ignoring the signs and going back to our comfort zone because familiarity is easy. The difficulty is standing firm in our beliefs and telling ourselves the right thing to do. How many times have you stopped talking to a significant other only to wait in loneliness and go back to what you knew wasn't good for you? How many times have you stayed when you had every reason to leave? You must always remember: you are alone, but never lonely. Don't become a creature of habit just because it seems like the easy way out.

    At one point, *The Artist* said he wanted to build something real with me—then he disappeared for over a week. I made it a habit not to reach out because I knew he wasn't ready for a woman like me. I always supported him and tried to give him friendship first, before anything, but he repeatedly took my kindness for weakness. When he finally reached out, he gave me a sorry response on not knowing why he did the things he did, and jumped ahead of himself with saying he was ready to build; but little did he know, I never took any of his propositions seriously. His actions always proved the total opposite of his words.

The Artist would get mad when I told him he didn't respect me, that he didn't value my time with his flakey nature; but secretly, I believe he knew I was right which was what caused his annoyance. When you tell people the reality of their actions they can't handle it. I was never in love with *The Artist*, but I will forever hold love in my heart for him because he taught me so many lessons. Because of him, I will never compromise my morals for another man and waste my time. He wasn't a bad guy and he was very sweet, but he was not my soul mate. *The Artist* was a soul tie that turned into a habit that was hard to kick because every time I felt myself becoming better, my insecurities about this single life made me go back to my safety net to pass time.

During this journey toward loving and valuing myself, I had to realize that I would never be fully happy or able to gain the capacity to love anyone without first loving myself completely. I had to love the girl who was often bullied and tortured by her older cousin who would sit on her while stuffing socks in her mouth; and the girl

The Commandments of Womanhood

who claimed she didn't need a man, but was secretly seeking validation in her worth by how much guys found her worthy of attention. Loving the little girl who had family members tell her she wasn't pretty enough because of her brown complexion and chocolate colored eyes was difficult, but it was something I needed to do.

There was a girl who used to get talked about at school; she would use a paper clip to cut into her skin in the back of the classroom, and I had to love her. The same girl that wished she jumped off the cruise boat instead of coming home to a room full of familiar strangers only to find out her mom wasn't really sick like people had misled her to believe, but dead, needed love. I had to love the girl that took 21 years to even kiss a man because she was afraid to be touched because of her having briefly being molested at day camp. She deserved love and she was worthy.

You are deserving and you are worthy. Everything that you have gone through up until this point has shaped you for the better—no matter how painful. We have to learn the lesson within each struggle. Everything molds us into our greater being. Nothing bad that has ever happened is working against you. It is up to you to learn how to recognize the blessing in every lesson.

    Getting to the bottom of why I felt like I needed drink to be myself was important for me. I was never a heavy or regular drinker, but every time I went out or was alone with a man I had to throw a few drinks back in order to let loose and be *myself*. I had to tell myself that my personality was and is good without the liquor courage. Have you ever found yourself doing things to feel better only feel worse the next day?

    Figuratively, as women, we often pour rubbing alcohol into our wounds rather than getting out the infections with peroxide first. I had to get to the bottom of everything that was holding me back. There was a decision that had to be made. The bags I was struggling to carry were too heavy and I had to set them down for good. Every day I changed the lies that I'd secretly told myself for years in order to create a new truth about me.

    The realization became evident that I had to love myself the way I wanted to be loved. If I didn't want unrequited love, then I had to stop merely giving my

The Commandments of Womanhood

love away without giving it to myself first. We often make excuses as to why it's so easy for us to do more for others while constantly shortchanging ourselves, but fail to realize that this ultimately sets the tone for what we receive.

Have you ever reasoned with yourself why you don't need that new item even though you haven't treated yourself in a while? In that same thought, you make no excuse to do that and more for another, for everyone else but you. Shortchanging yourself all the time can eventually lead you to feeling unappreciated and resentful. Giving freely isn't just about how much you can give to others, but also what you can give to yourself. You have to go above and beyond for yourself instead of waiting for someone else to. Self-care is remembering to replenish yourself as you give to the world. Recognizing this made me choose to do more for myself.

Finding new books to read inspired my new train of thought. With conditioning your mind, you must also learn to embrace body positivity. Remember that this is your body. The flaws, stretch marks, blemishes, cellulite, and scars belong to you. Own them and love them. Stand in front of the mirror naked constantly and admire the curves that create the makeup of your outer being. This is what you are working with, so learn to love every piece of you.

Feed your mind with things that will lift you up and inspire you like books and positive music. Take a step back from the world and take a step into loving you. Distance yourself from social media and constant negativity. You have a choice as to what you subject yourself to; don't get distracted by what's going on around you. Take yourself on dates, and instead of documenting your life with pictures and public posts, write about it in a place that is only for your eyes. Reflect and acknowledge everything that you are going through, and express how you feel inside. If you can't be honest with anybody else, at least be honest with yourself.

More importantly you must forgive yourself. You can't forgive anyone else if you don't even believe the past indiscretions that you committed against yourself are worthy of forgiveness. There is no better love than

The Commandments of Womanhood

God's love and the love you give yourself. You can't find your soul mate if your soul is not whole. Become your first soul mate. You owe yourself that and so much more. As women, we tend to be our own worst critics. Don't be so hard on yourself. We all make mistakes. We all hurt, encounter loss, and experience pain. Give yourself time to heal. There is no manual that can help you become the perfect woman. It's not only hard being a woman, but sometimes it's just hard to wake up in the morning. Always be honest with yourself and acknowledge your mistakes, but don't regret anything. Learn from your mistakes and allow it to help you to grow and become the amazing woman that God has called you to be.

    Don't wait for someone else to validate the beauty within you. It is up to you to create such a powerful mindset that whether they are celebrating with you or trying to tear you down, your mind remains made up. You should know that you are the best thing since sliced bread; and whoever is trying to be with you should be honored that you are bestowing the beauty of your presence around them.

The Commandments of Womanhood

The Commandments of Womanhood

Protect Thy Energy

As women, we must be especially mindful of the company we keep. A woman's energy is by far one of the most sacred things she has to offer. Allowing tainted souls around your energy can have a sneaky way of slithering in and damaging your aura. Nobody can make you feel anything without you first giving him or her permission to do so. We as women must learn that we do not have the ability to change anyone other than ourselves. A lot of times we feel responsible for bringing out the good in others that they fail to bring about within themselves. Although we have the ability to spark a change within someone, the change can only take affect if the other party is willing and open.

You can lead horses to water, but you cannot make them drink. We must stop trying to make it our duty to change our mates. We as women often make excuses for intolerable acts that we allow. The change sparked within another person has to be a choice that

The Commandments of Womanhood

they made themselves. This logic can be applied to friendships and any other relationships. Stressing ourselves over damaged, unhealthy souls is not healthy for our mind and spirit. Surrounding ourselves with people who have unbalanced energy can cause a shift within our entire being. Have you ever started off having a great day, but noticed how your energy is shifted once you come in contact with a negative person? Your energy is as beautiful and as delicate as your mind, and it should be treated with care.

Giving too much energy to useless situations will burn you out. Sometimes it's best to just observe and move on. They say: "Show me whom you surround yourself with and I'll tell you who you are." The people whom you surround yourself with is not something that can or should be taken lightly no matter who they are. We should always become aware of the energies that surround us as well as our own. Negative people and situations are not worth giving your energy to. When you feed into those kinds of situations you let others drain the best parts of you.

The Commandments of Womanhood

Never grant another person enough power over you to break your spirit and tarnish your beautifully glowing energy. A constant reminder one should keep in mind when facing life's many obstacles is if it's not for the advancement of your energy and evolution, then it has to go. Balance out what is worth your energy and the things that are just bringing out the worst in you. Life has a way of making the repetitious cycles that bind us feel like Groundhog's Day unless we fight through the trials that hold us captive and overcome.

There are so many different blessings in the lessons we encounter. When we continue to put our energy into the same situations, we will continue to get the same results unless a shift in our actions is made. Life is all about getting over strongholds and progressing. Learn lessons and let them be your strength. You have the power; you are as strong as you allow yourself to become. If we continue to fall victim to the very things that constantly drain our energy, we will never progress or, more importantly, become the person we were destined to be.

The Commandments of Womanhood

Life is all about choices. It's so important to be mindful of the things and people you choose to share your energy with for it takes twice as long to cleanse yourself of the toxic waste that you have been exposed to. Soul ties are real; so don't share your soul with just anybody because your soul is not for everybody. Protect yourself; don't neglect yourself.

The Commandments of Womanhood

The Commandments of Womanhood

Rule Thy Happiness

Quest to becoming happy and unpacking your bags

"I had fainted, unless I had believed to see the goodness of the Lord in the land of the living. Wait on the Lord: be of good courage, and he shall strengthen thine heart: wait, I say, on the Lord". *Psalms 27:13-14*

Happiness is your birthright and you are deserving of it. This was a lesson that personally took me about 8+ years to grasp. Life for me hadn't been the easiest and I had a bad habit of keeping my bags both physically and emotionally packed. I constantly guarded myself and refused to connect with others. Subconsciously, I'd built a shell around my entire being. I didn't allow myself to build connections with others for the fear of loss.

Mentally, I'd paralyzed myself from gaining the capacity to love another because of the numerous loved

The Commandments of Womanhood

ones I lost during the fundamental years of my adolescence. The two major deaths were of both my parents, which happened 7 years apart. I developed a habit of distancing myself from people when I felt them getting too close. This defense mechanism caused me years of loneliness and isolation, making me miss out on teen dating as well as new friendships. My inability to love and be happy hardened me like it does so many other women. We as women should be warm, full of love and happiness. We all deserve happiness regardless of our circumstances or shortcomings.

About two years ago I allowed myself to get stuck working for a company that almost stole my happiness. At the start of working for this company, I had so much promise. At 19 years old, I was a first time published author, had a newly started clothing line that was growing buzz, and a passion for photography and film that was beginning to peak. The longer I worked for this company the more I began to lose focus on what was important to me as well as what I was working towards.

This was supposed to be temporary and I had allowed myself to become complacent. I wasn't booking

The Commandments of Womanhood

with my photography anymore and I even stopped designing clothes. My rise to greatness was short lived at 20. At 21 years old, I found myself extremely depressed because the once competitive pay from my job at the time had been reduced substantially. It had gotten so bad to where I would drink a gallon of water a day just to remain nourished because I had to miss several meals throughout the week. I had to eventually take on a second job and I was blessed that it ended up being a restaurant.

I would wake up at 5 AM after only getting home via public transportation at 4:30 AM from working two jobs just to do it all over again. One time I got off so late that I literally had to sleep at the train station while it was freezing because I missed the last train home. I didn't sleep that day; instead I took a shower and changed clothes to go back to work.

Physically and mentally I was killing myself, so much so that it nearly made me delirious. I could remember going to my full time job and crying with my head down on a desk in the back of the office because I was so tired. My bills just seemed to keep piling up and

The Commandments of Womanhood

even with the added stress of working two jobs I still didn't manage to make enough money to cover all my expenses. This was not a life worth living and I did not want to die miserable. We are not meant to merely live to die. Life is all about living a full prosperous life and dying empty because you have accomplished all the things that you wanted to while adding something of substance to the world. There is no greater satisfaction than living a fulfilled and happy life. Consciously, I had to make the decision to let my part time job at the restaurant go before I lost my full time job at the satellite company. I was beginning to be spread too thin.

Throughout the time I worked at my full time job, I would constantly fill job applications only to get turned away. When I say I filled out several jobs applications I mean literally around a hundred a day, but it seemed as though I just couldn't get anywhere. With every interview, my faith began to deteriorate as I got hit with another no. I felt trapped within a job I hated and my life was miserable. I couldn't believe what had become of my life because I knew I had more to offer the world than simply staying at a 9 to 5. Living to just pay bills,

The Commandments of Womanhood

be in debt, and die could not be my life. Although I hardly allowed myself to be consumed by emotion, I can honestly say this period of my life saw so many tears. A couple of weeks after resigning from my job at the restaurant, I lost my job at the satellite company. Here I was, now freshly 22 and unemployed the week before Christmas. How ironic to resign from my part time job so I wouldn't lose my full time income only to end up losing my full time job a few weeks later.

    Little did I know, getting laid off would probably become one of the best things that ever happened to me. This event ended up being the beginning of a chain reaction that would shift my entire life and mindset. *Your life will begin to change once you begin to change your mind.* As I heard the news, it was like a weight had been lifted off my shoulders. When I received my last check, something in me suddenly clicked. Walking out of the building smiling widely, I knew that everything would be just fine. Something within me made me know that everything would be handled. That something was God.

    As I left that chapter of depression behind, I made a mental vow to myself that I would never work at

The Commandments of Womanhood

another job that made me unhappy. If they could so easily throw me away after begging me to stay only a few months prior, I could never bring myself to stay somewhere for so long that didn't appreciate me. Realizing my worth in the work place was important because I was starting to realize that everything was temporary. These jobs could no longer have the ability to work me because I began to work them.

    How dare I become complacent and lose focus of my purpose? One of my fears had come to pass which helped me become more fearless and unafraid. *When we let go of fear, amazing things begin to happen.* Always afraid of not having a plan, I was obsessed with order. There was always a need to feel I was in control of my life; and while it is good to have plans, do not become so blinded by them that you don't focus on living to your full potential. *Life is all about choices and the mindset you have while facing adversity.* The crazy thing is that I stumbled upon an interview the next day, and on Christmas Eve I found out that I'd been hired for a position with a company that paid twice as much as my previous job. *What you think about, you bring about.*

The Commandments of Womanhood

If you have the mindset that you can get any job you put your mind to, you will do just that. The only thing left to worry about is if you will actually allow yourself to have it. How hard are you willing to work for your goal until it's accomplished? Since being let go from the satellite company, I have left two other companies on my own terms. Each job I have gotten since has paid more than the last. *Instead of fighting against the tide, I began to embrace it and flow within it.* Change is inevitable. Although we have control over some areas of our lives, we have to learn as people that it is okay not to always be in control. The faster we learn to become adaptable, the easier it will become to face unforeseen obstacles with a positive mindset.

My quest for happiness was and still is important. The pursuit of happiness is a quest that continues because even once obtained it has to be maintained. One day I woke up and realized I wasn't sad anymore. After finding peace within how I made my money, I had to connect that same mindset and apply it to my life personally. Money doesn't equate to happiness; and with new levels we start to run into new devils. You can be

The Commandments of Womanhood

financially at your highest, but mentally at your lowest. All areas of our lives are equally as important and should be balanced. Smiling and laughing more was a key factor in this change within me.

For the longest time I couldn't fathom how to execute being happy. It was as if I were subconsciously telling myself that because I so damaged, I wasn't deserving of happiness. I had to sit down with myself and write all the things that I feared to ever utter aloud as well as everything that continued to hold me back. The thing that I noticed when I made that list of my fears is that all my fears were secretly wants that I was afraid to allow myself to have. Sometimes the only thing that is truly holding you back from peace, love, happiness, and abundance is yourself.

It should be a sin to purposely sabotage yourself from getting the life you want. What are the things that you are afraid to allow yourself to want? Is it security, consistency, wealth, success, or happiness? I had a fear of vulnerability, romantic commitment, loss, and building with others. My past had paralyzed me to a point that I didn't even want to get married or have

The Commandments of Womanhood

children for the fear of loving someone so much only to lose them again. Fear can stagnate your growth if you let it consume you.

Losing people is inevitable and emotions are natural. Once you acknowledge fears rather than suppress them, you can gain the strength to overcome. So many people feel a particular way without acknowledging their feelings. It is not enough to just feel. *You must become, absorb, digest, process, and whatever else you need to do in order to overcome the obstacle.*

We dwell so much in sadness and end up consumed in depression because of denial. You are allowed to have emotions and digest whatever it is that you are feeling in order to connect with it. *The moment we choose to ignore how we feel is the exact moment we ignite the fire within that feeling to grow into something we ultimately will not be able to contain.* By holding on and not releasing, we make our journey so much harder than it needs to be in the first place. Your feelings are valid and don't let anyone ever tell you otherwise.

The Commandments of Womanhood

Acknowledge the validity of your emotions and overcome them.

After getting that job things, turned around for me, but sadly that was not the end of my trial. I resigned from two jobs after being fired from the call center. Jobs are like shoes: You've got to sometimes try a few out to see what works for you. The main thing to remember when getting a job is to never get complacent. Your purpose is bigger than your current situation. Do not get side tracked on the things that don't matter. Jobs are beneficial for the meantime, but make them work for you instead of simply working for them. The trick is to work smarter not harder.

If you take the job route before walking into your purpose, make sure to do something that is secure enough to get you where you want to go and allows you the time to get things done for you too. Life is full of two types of people: those who live their purpose and those that work in order to make someone else's dream happen. What type of person will you become? At least if you are going to the second one temporarily, make sure it's working for you too. You owe yourself that at all cost. Work the system; don't let it work you. We all have to start from somewhere and for me I had to get a job because I didn't have the luxury of having a safety net while pursuing my passion.

I finally found the perfect job that allowed me to work from home while getting back to me. After working at this job for a couple of months, I found myself bored yet again so I started being productive. I'd find a good book to read and meal prep between taking calls at home. I started changing my eating habits and changing how I cared for myself. Keeping my apartment clean was a big thing for me as well because I figured I had to get ready for the mansion that I claimed to want for myself.

We always want so much out of life, but fail to value what we have before fixing our mouths to ask God for more. I don't know about you, but I did that all the time. How can you want a house when you can't even take care of your apartment? People want cars, but leave trash on the trains they ride. You have to live the way you feel you should be living before you get it and thank God in advance for His promise. God isn't a genie, but a

The Commandments of Womanhood

provider who already knows what you want before you open your mouth. Stop asking God for things and start thanking Him for everything He's already done. Gratitude is important to finding happiness because if you remember where you've been and where God brought you, the little things that you think you need immediately no longer matter.

    A great passage that can depict this is Matthew 6:7-8 which reads "But when ye pray, use not vain repetitions, as the heathens do for they think that they shall be heard for their much speaking. Be not ye therefore like unto them: for your father knoweth what things ye have need of, before ye ask him." Faith is a walk and mentality. You have to know without a shadow of doubt that everything you believe will come into fruition. Trust in God's promise and watch Him work it out on your behalf. It took me years to learn that it's better to walk with Him than try to take in on by yourself.

    The quest to happiness and getting everything you want in life begins with believing that you are deserving of it all. Believe that it's possible and, like the

The Commandments of Womanhood

Bible says, believe that everything you want is already done. By living as though I had everything I wanted another shift began that took me on yet another crazy roller coaster. I stumbled upon my purpose. When I stumbled upon my purpose I was afraid and taken aback because I felt that I wasn't worthy of such a big task. How was this broken young woman going to help so many women? I felt unworthy of such a huge and divine task.

When I decided to write this book, I didn't know where I was going with this. Once I started, I was on a roll. This book idea started off as a question to my followers and friends on social media: What are the things that you believe every woman should know? I was taken aback again by the response that I received and it started to get my creative juices flowing. This concept made me think about the things I'd want to tell a younger sister or a daughter. This was a handbook that I felt like every young woman should have while making the transition into adulthood. I wrote what I thought at the time was the complete manuscript which ended up only being the skeleton of the testimony that would soon

The Commandments of Womanhood

evolve in these pages. The next 8 months were so trying and I figured out that I was missing the God factor within these pages.

God had other plans for the inspirational pocketbook that I thought I was writing. To say I had high hopes for the success of this book was taking things extremely lightly because I had high realities. I made it a point to stop calling the things I wanted out of life dreams because they might get stuck there. I saw book tours and conferences. I saw so much in a 30-page pocket book, but there was so much more that needed to be written.

Be careful what you ask God for because the crazy thing is you might actually get it. I made a virtual vision board this year and on it I wrote I wanted to get a new place, help people build their dreams, inspire and motivate my loved ones, create, write, pray more, unplug from the world, stay consistent with my health (hair, skin, and body), build my credit back up, save, and a few more things that don't really matter anymore to me. I had the bright idea to put it on my phone as a screen saver

The Commandments of Womanhood

because that way I could think about it subconsciously more than ever and manifest it into reality.

I didn't know I was asking for more work than I thought I had to do which initially halted my happiness party. With getting things together in my apartment, I decided to finally get everything fixed that I was too busy working previously to acknowledge. In the 2+ years that I lived in my apartment, I never called maintenance and put in a ticket. Before I go into the rest of this story I should probably start at the beginning of how I even got my first apartment.

When I first got somewhat on my own I ended up renting a two-bedroom apartment with a girl that was a friend of my best friend. My best friend's coworker from a previous job was renting a room and her roommate moved out without telling her. She needed a new roommate because she didn't want to break her lease and ruin her credit more than she already had. When initially being presented with the idea, I was hesitant because moving in with a somewhat stranger made me iffy. At this time, we all worked together at a call center, but the girl and me were neither close nor that cool. My home situation eventually became unbearable so I decided to jump at the opportunity to be on my own. My roommate eventually did the same thing her roommate did to her and moved out abruptly on her birthday. The only difference is she told me after she was already gone by sending me a text message when she didn't come back for weeks while on her birthday trip. The apartment was not in my name, but it didn't stop me from freaking out at first because I assumed I'd be homeless.

    My apartment manager at the time assured me no harm would come to me and she would allow to stay until the lease ended while only paying my portion of the rent. The manager respected that I paid on time and she allowed me to move into a one bedroom after the lease was completed to finish off another tenant's lease. As you read that sentence again notice how I said she allowed me when I should've been saying God allowed me. The bigger picture is that God allowed me to go through smooth transitions and continued to present doors even when I failed to give Him the first thanks. Don't get me wrong, I always thanked God when opportunities were given, but I failed to see His full hand

The Commandments of Womanhood

in everything. God really shook this into me during the 3 years of my life that this book chronicles.

    Now that I gave you the back-story on how I really got my apartment, let me get back to telling you the rest of this story. I went ahead and got my unit fixed. Randomly a few weeks later, I received an alarming call from my apartment manager freaking out. The company that was over the building found out that I was not an official resident when the previous tenant informed them that she hadn't been living there in several years. This came about after she was followed up with a survey from the maintenance department. Keep in mind the tenant met me, knew I was going to take over her lease, and even left me furniture which baffled me as to why she would tell them the truth. Read that sentence again. I was baffled that she told them the truth. The Lord will never put you in a deceitful position when He blesses you, but He will have favor over your life. God had His hand upon me, and His favor allowed me to keep this place as long as I did.

    Listen to me when I tell you—what God has for you no one can take. His real blessings are never

The Commandments of Womanhood

borrowed nor will they be able to be so easily taken—which I found out in the months that followed. My manager assured me that she'd call and get to the bottom of everything so I could stay, so I remained hopeful. Once again, I placed my hope in a person other than my Father who had been keeping me since before I was thought of.

    A week goes by and I'm nervous, but I continue to tell myself everything will be just fine and remained hopeful. My apartment manager at the time calls me up and told me that the previous tenant had unconsciously sent a message to be unsubscribed from notifications because she didn't live in the unit. It had been so long since she lived there that she forgot about me subleasing her unit. The girl felt so bad because she didn't want me to get put out and confirmed that it was never her intention since I helped her not break her lease. She had forgotten about the apartment until I my manager called her. Again my manager convinced me that everything would be resolved and I did not have to worry. Once again I continue putting my trust in a person instead of putting my trust in the Lord.

The Commandments of Womanhood

My manager goes on to tell me that we would just need to switch the place into my name. When she finally called me over to her place she told me I had to complete paper work online, but that is was not an official application. I had to pay a fee and I asked was she sure it wasn't the real application because I didn't want my credit ran. She goes on to say they will not run my credit without notifying her first and that although it was an application they wouldn't treat it as such since I had been living there for a little over 2 years.

  The next day my manager called me and told she had bad news. She said the owners were giving me until the end of the next month to move out. I held it together and once I released the end button on my phone I wept like a baby. I threw the biggest tantrum and cursed God. Anger was not even the half of what I was feeling. I finally had a great job and was coming into what I felt was my purpose. My relationship with God was growing to what it once was and I felt like I'd been obedient to Him with the direction my life was going. I had just written what I felt was such a powerful book that would change my life and here I was homeless. I literally went into debt, ruined my credit, sacrificed bills, and took out several payday loans just to keep this apartment. I starved for that apartment and now I was back at square one with no place to go. Just when I finally got comfortable enough to start unpacking for the first time in 8 years, both literally and figuratively, here I was packing again. I had stopped drinking hard liquor at the time, but I was so depressed I needed something to numb the blow.

    I walked to the liquor store and grabbed me a bottle of flavored vodka and large bottle of wine. I couldn't bring myself to drink the vodka, but I drank the whole bottle of wine. Eventually I called my best friend/sister Niko and she gave it to me straight; she told me what I needed to do while trying to formulate a plan for me. I had no savings or safety net, so trying to keep up with paying current rent and getting money to move somewhere seemed like an impossible task. Niko's logic and tough love in my time of despair made me absolutely furious. I told her I would call her back because in the almost suicidal state I was in I didn't want tough love.

The Commandments of Womanhood

I've always managed to hold it together so that even when I'm close to edge, nobody knows. In that moment I just needed to vent and for once give into all my emotions. If only for a second, I had to stop being the strong girl who had to plan her mom's funeral at 15. I just needed a minute to be emotional. I texted my pregnant friend Dyamond and she offered to come over. Honestly, I felt like giving up that day and it was only God's grace that kept me. Dyme came over and she sat in my bed with me. We listened to the sweet melodies of Anita Baker and stared at the wall as she comforted me while my tears fell repeatedly without my permission.

    Many will probably wonder why this situation made me so angry and sad, but when you don't have any parents or grandparents, the safety net you no longer have makes you paranoid. When you realize that you have nowhere to fall because you can't catch yourself this time it feels so discouraging, especially when you've worked so hard for everything you have. All I knew was taking care of myself for years even before living on my own. After my mom passed away, I had to up my independence and handle a lot of things you'd assume an adult would. It seemed like when I finally became fully independent on my own, my failure made me feel like I was going to drown this time. Little did I know God was going to catch me repeatedly and put me in so many uncomfortable positions so that when it was all over I would give Him the ultimate praise. Depression is the insidious thoughts that we often ignore. The strongest people have felt weak and sometimes that trigger that can seem small for one person becomes the tip of the iceberg for another.

    Instead of giving my troubles to God, I went into survival mode and made so many irrational compromises over the next 8 months. I had a friend at the time that was also having some hard times so I asked if he was still looking for a roommate to help split the cost of his rent with him. He told me he was and the rest was history. To be honest, I was actually excited because I felt like our struggle would bring us even closer, however, this living situation ultimately drove us apart. I guess it's true what they say, you never really know a person until you live with them.

The Commandments of Womanhood

When initially going into this situation, I knew that it would be a struggle living with two young men in a small studio apartment in Korea Town, but I was up for the challenge. In my mind this period would be filled with us motivating and inspiring each other. The funny thing is the struggle of it all was the real blessing.

My friend Rochelle offered to help me move and I put the majority of my belongings in storage. The first day I moved in with the guys it was so positive and we danced while the guys made me feel so welcomed. I worked from home doing customer care and I had to answer calls. Prior to moving in with my friend and his homeboy, I had only visited his place maybe twice. We went to church together and went places from time to time, but we never hung with each other on a consistent basis. When we did link up it was always love and when we texted each other it was mainly to uplift each other so we only saw the good in each other during our year of friendship prior to me moving in.

My friend at the time was very well known within the social media community so he was very popular and always out networking. During the

The Commandments of Womanhood

beginning of my stay he worked a lot at a new creative content company, so that also added to me not seeing him much. When the company disbanded and he was let go, I began to see more and more of him, which is when the problems came. As time went on, our honeymoon roommate stage subdued and my irritation level was through the roof. I never realized that as a social media personality my friend had no off switch for the person he portrayed online. The same over the top personality that made me laugh in the beginning began to clash with my mellow introverted one.

    From the obnoxious allergy noises all day to the constant loud off key singing during the times when I was working and talking to customers over the phone, I nearly went nuts. There were times that I'd be on the Skype with my manager and the two guys I stayed with would be play fighting while cursing loudly in the background putting my job at risk. There was literally never a moment of silence while my friend was home.

    His friend wasn't working and pretty much living rent free for the first two months without really bothering to look for a job. I felt it was unfair because my friend

The Commandments of Womanhood

and I paid rent while his friend sat on the phone all day talking about insignificance while being lazy. His lack of work ethic was something that I could not comprehend because I had been starting my own businesses since 16 and I've always been a go-getter. The longer I lived with them, the more annoyed at my situation I became. This made me lose sight of the reason I thought living together would be so amazing in the first place.

Eventually, just being in that non-motivating environment began to take a toll on me. I constantly found myself losing patience. They were both junky and rarely cleaned after themselves. After observing their cleaning habits, I made it a point to myself that I would not clean after them because I refused to be their maid. I would straighten the area where I slept on my friend's air mattress and make sure I cleaned after what I used. If I wasn't working, I tried to sleep through it because I hated living in an unclean home. As a creative person I couldn't focus in a room full of chaos and junk.

My friend did clean occasionally when he felt like it, but when he did he made it like he was doing the house such a big service when he merely just cleaned the mess he made. Eventually I started to going over to Dyme's house every chance I got to help her get ready for the arrival of her daughter and get away from my roommates. I didn't like conflict, so instead of addressing my feelings I just stayed to myself. When I addressed anything, my friend's combative nature made me want to hold myself reserved before I said something I'd regret. When my niece Marz was born, I'd sometimes spend 4 days to a week at Dyme's house to help lighten her load, and also get away from the tension that always found its way into the apartment.

I could feel at times they didn't like me, so I tried to stay out of the way. Maybe it was the slight age difference, but the longer I stayed the more I realized we were just different people. There were so many times when my friend would make me feel welcomed, only to then quickly let me know he doesn't need me there even though he was drowning in bills. I never felt completely comfortable and it showed in my actions. Although there were a lot of bad times with the tension and negativity, there were some good times as well. I began to let my situation and environment control my mind, and even

The Commandments of Womanhood

though a friendship was lost during this time, I still appreciate having a roof over my head during that time.

My friend went home for a few weeks before I moved out; and prior to the weeks leading up to him visiting his hometown, we were cool—before he became distant. A few days before he left, the air mattress his friend gave him, which I was using, popped. I was forced to sleep on a hard twin-sized mattress on the floor. It was so hard that the metal prongs from the springs began digging into my back, making it hard for me to sleep. Regardless of my comfort level, I was still just thankful to at least have a place to stay. This period was definitely a culture shock because I'd never lived in an environment such as this in the past.

Leading up to me moving out, I began noticing more and more of the roaches that my friend had assured me he didn't have prior to me choosing to move in. Little did I know, he just didn't know what roaches looked like in California and had mistaken them for water bugs. I'd never lived with roaches, so I was just taken aback. Eventually, after sleeping on the mattress for a week, a roach crawled on me in my sleep—and that's when I had

The Commandments of Womanhood

it. This utterly repulsed me to say the least. I didn't sleep the rest of that night. After taking a hot shower, I stayed up until Starbucks opened. I stayed at Starbucks until the sun came up and then went to my friend Lakeisha's apartment in Lakewood. She allowed me to spend the night and I was extremely grateful because I was able to get the first good night's rest in over a week.

During the last two weeks before moving out, I began visiting my dad's sister and keeping her company. I applied for an apartment that I just knew I would get that wasn't too far from her house. While at the apartment, I began sleeping on my friend's futon since his friend was sleeping on his bed while he was out of town. Sleeping on the futon his friend usually slept in ended up giving me welts and bites all over, but in my mind anything was better than having roaches crawling on me in my sleep.

I feel like when God was getting ready to take me out of the uncomfortable situation, the weeks leading up to that seemed more unbearable than the 4 months that I'd lived there. I made up my mind that I was moving regardless of if I found a place or not because I

The Commandments of Womanhood

couldn't take anymore bugs or negativity. The news of my denial for the apartment came the day before I was scheduled to move out. My friend at the time was still in his hometown.

    The day before I moved out, he reached out, and because things had been so tense leading up to him going to his hometown, I was almost hesitant to even reply because I felt our friendship might've been damaged beyond repair. He asked me about my luck on my apartment search and I let him know I didn't find anything but I was still going to leave the next day as agreed upon. When I thanked him for letting me stay, he began revealing his masked ill-feelings toward me. I initially wanted to extend an olive branch to try and salvage the friendship we had prior, but the way the conversation shifted made my Kumbaya go out the window.

    The passive aggressive nature in which he approached me stung, and, in true Scorpio fashion, my pride made me let him know his dislike for me at times was a mutual thing. He would say things like I'm so sweet and positive only to insult my character with

The Commandments of Womanhood

negativity after each compliment. Most of the things he praised me for when meeting me, he began to dislike about me. He wasn't the person I thought he was and my intuition about his true feelings for me became clear in the end. He even went as far as using a conversation I told him in confidence about a guy I was talking to and tried to morph that conversation into his opinion about me.

    Instead of burning the bridge beyond compare, I decided to humble myself while holding my reserve. Previously, I had been asking God to humble me, so I don't give every action my reaction and I was proud of myself for holding it together. During my entire stay I'd been battling between who I wanted to be and who God wanted me to be. Moments when I felt myself becoming cold would quickly end with me apologizing because I didn't want to be the old me. I was even going to still be nice and leave him all of my dishes, but when he continued to use sarcastic jabs I decided not to give anything to a person that repeatedly insulted my character. Giving gifts while holding hostility to someone can make you be resentful, so instead of

The Commandments of Womanhood

holding that type of space I gave my pots, pan, dishes, and crockpot to his apartment manager and a man fixing the elevator downstairs.

After moving out of the apartment, I found myself in a hotel and my friend Rochelle helped me move yet again. It was bitter sweet, but I decided to make the most of it after a conversation with my friend Jessica from high school. I had thought about just taking the money I'd saved to start over in a different state, but she helped me see that starting over wouldn't make a difference, and at least here I had a good job. My mind was always in survival mode, but this season taught me that I couldn't run from all my problems.

The next day after a great catch up conversation with my friend from high school, I treated myself to an expensive nail day. I even went shopping—which I hadn't done in years. It felt great to get back to treating myself and loving on me. I was no longer being frugal with myself and I promised myself I would start taking better care of me because I worked too hard to live an unfulfilled life. When I got back to my hotel room, I gave myself a facial and deep conditioned my hair while

The Commandments of Womanhood

feeling lavish in a bug free environment. I had an amazing week of sleep. After that weekend, I went to another hotel in Anaheim.

On the 4th of July, I decided to take my aunt up on her offer to stay with her since I soon realized that living in a hotel is way more expensive than I had hoped. I was happy to be back around my family and I felt like this was God's way of bringing me back around. Before I moved in with my aunt, my wonderful best friend Niko allowed me to stay with her for a week so I could save money instead of extending my hotel room.

While living with my aunty, I'd manage to bring my cousin back around more who'd become distant after a nervous breakdown. We all have our own demons that we battle and my cousin was always quiet when it came to hers, so I understood her breakdown as a way of God telling her to slow down. My cousin was the baby of her siblings and as she got older her parents weren't as financially secure as they once were with her older siblings. This ultimately made her choose to work harder in silence so she wouldn't have to burden anyone.

The Commandments of Womanhood

My cousin and I, being 6 days apart, had always had each other's back since birth. When I didn't have groceries in my apartment she brought me food; and when she wasn't working I had her back as well. It had always been this way, and even though we talked less than we did as children, our bond always remained the same because she was more of a sister to me than a cousin. I told her the things I was afraid to even admit to myself sometimes.

I admired her resilience so much because she has the most calming and gentle soul I'd ever encountered. As women, we tend to carry the world on our shoulders and never ask for help. Mental illness is real and we drive ourselves there when we overwork and stop listening to the things our body tells us. Battling mental health was something I knew well because in the past I struggled with often being depressed while isolating myself.

Things seemed like they were finally looking up. I was able to help my aunty with the kids she had taken in and more importantly spend time with my family. I didn't get to see them as much within the last 2 years

The Commandments of Womanhood

because I had started working so much. A couple of friends that I thought I was close to became distant during this time, but at least I felt like I had my family to count on. I felt like I was able to really talk to my aunt and let her know how I was feeling about being 23 living place to place. She had so much wisdom and she let me know that I was still young and we all fall sometimes.

My aunt told me that I was way too hard on myself, and family will always be there to take care of each other. I appreciated her motherly love during the time when it seemed like I was beginning to miss my mom more than ever. During this time, I was able to unload the emotional bags that I found myself picking up again, and this time I wanted to set them down for good. I let my aunt know that my stay would be no more than 6 months max, unlike when I stayed with her after coming home from my first year of college for 2 years. She let me know I could stay as long as I needed and she actually tried to convince me to just stay forever.

Once again, just when I felt comfort in being around family, things took a turn for the worst. We had a family trip to help my older cousin with the arrival of his

The Commandments of Womanhood

new baby. I was super excited because he was another cousin who was more like an older brother because Anesa, Greg, and I grew up together very close because my dad and his sister lived close to each other. The trip was initially supposed to be my cousin/sister, my aunt, and I. Family drama got in the way, which caused my aunt to feel more comfortable if she were to take the little girl that she took in, who was quite the handful, with us.

When we arrived in Chicago everything started off great. However, slowly, but surely, the stress of our trip and my aunt's anxiety began to make her moody, especially with the little girl around. She was a lot to deal with at times because she had a smart mouth and didn't listen. Kids will be kids, and sometimes we tend to forget that kids who've had mothers who did drugs throughout their entire pregnancy need more patience and understanding. Everyone's nerves were on edge with trying to get everything ready for the new baby and the fact that there were 7 people in a two-bedroom home didn't make it better. My cousin Anesa, my cousin's wife Brandy who was expecting, and I decided to go get

The Commandments of Womanhood

food after dealing with the little girl all day. As we walked out she threw tantrum because she wanted to go with us; I assumed she'd get over it, so we proceeded to leave.

My aunt got mad and accused me of slamming the door in the girl's face, which was not intentional. I simply closed the door gently behind myself. My aunt thought it was better if the child went and I didn't, so instead of arguing and making things worse, I decided to stay. I took a nap since I wasn't feeling too well to begin with. When they got back after getting snacks, they asked me if I was going to cook and I declined. After sitting for a minute, I decided not to let the pettiness dampen my time so I decided to cook and went in the kitchen to prepare one of the meals we planned earlier that week. That night my aunt decided not to eat because I cooked. Regardless, she was and still is my favorite aunt, and I love her despite her moodiness.

Later that night my cousin, my aunt, and I were watching television while I was still giving my aunt her space to cool down, so I tried not to force conversation. The show we were watching ran out of episodes so my

The Commandments of Womanhood

cousin and I decided to figure out what to watch next. Out of nowhere, my aunt flipped out and began yelling at the top her lungs at 2 AM saying that I changed what she was watching. My cousin and I tried to reason with her that the episodes had gone off and there were no more episodes on demand, but she made up her mind that I was the enemy. I offered my aunt the remote and she refused. Sitting the remote on the ground next to the couch, I took out my laptop to watch shows to avoid any further confrontation. Moments later, my aunt became irate and began yelling at me again, accusing me of throwing the remote at her. This was after she got tired of watching a blank screen while being petty because she refused to take the remote when I offered it to her.

    I knew it was deeper than leaving the little girl earlier or the show going off so I probed to understand why she was so angry with me. I remained calmed and tried to reason with her, but there was no use because my aunt was on the warpath. She began to hit me where it hurt the most, which was far below the belt. She repeatedly threw everything I told her in confidence in my face and began asking questions about my living

The Commandments of Womanhood

situation that she knew the answers to. I remained strong and didn't argue back with her; instead I tried to be the voice of reason. The only thing that got her to calm down was my older cousin coming out the room asking her to stop because he had to wake up in an hour.

That night, as I stared in the dark texting my cousin Anesa who sat across from me, I couldn't help but feel so hurt as the hot tears cascaded down my cheeks. My entire life we had to endure my aunt's mood swings because of her bipolar disorder. Instead of telling her when she was wrong, our family had a certain way that we dealt with her. Although I knew she had her own mental issues, the things she said still stung. Once again, I felt like just when I allowed myself to open up and be vulnerable it came back to bite me.

The next day she still wasn't speaking to me and was giving me the cold shoulder. I decided I was going to have fun and still enjoy myself with hopes that she'd come around, so I tried to stay out of her way. She took jabs about me all day and made it unbearable for everyone to have a good time because it was so tense. The more we stayed in the house the more remarks were

The Commandments of Womanhood

indiscreetly made in reference to me. I stayed quiet and out of the house most of the day in order to keep the peace.

It was supposed to be a happy time for my cousin's wife, and to see her uncomfortable in her own home broke my heart. I tried to mend things, but my aunt's stubbornness made that impossible. My cousin's wife broke down because of the tension. This was the first child she was having without her mom being alive, and that made me even sadder since we were both motherless women. It even made me fear having children in the future because I didn't want to go through this during the time surrounding the birth of a child. Later that night, the issue still wasn't resolved. I had hoped that it would wind down since my aunt was drinking her favorite wine, but things got worse.

While in the living room on Snapchat, I overheard my cousins laughing and talking with my aunt in the kitchen. She kept making indirect remarks about not wanting me here and asking my cousin to stay with her longer on the trip. It felt like she literally picked open the scabs from scars that had taken me years to heal only

The Commandments of Womanhood

to pour hot rubbing alcohol on them. No matter how old you become, not having living parents and feeling unwanted never seems to fully leave the back of your mind.

    Eventually she had enough of me staying to myself and once again picked another argument with me over what I was watching on my phone saying it was too loud. By this time, I had enough of the pettiness. Our whole lives we have excused her actions because of her mental state and it wasn't fair. Being passive was no longer cutting it so I came straight out with it. I asked her why she continued picking fights with me when I was not bothering anyone and just staying to myself. She had been taken jabs at me all day as well as the previous night, so turning the cheek after being cursed out repeatedly was no longer an option for me. My whole life I had been passive when it came to confrontational people. I wanted answers, and even with my questions, I remained respectful and refrained from speaking the way I wanted to—which was like a sailor. I wanted to blow up, but I still held some of my composure.

The Commandments of Womanhood

No one had ever really questioned her during her moody moments so my questions made her angry. She told me I was hard to live with which was ironic because back home in California she'd always say how things were so much easier with me staying with her. She called me disrespectful and then went on to say that when I got back to California, I had to find somewhere else to live. My pride wouldn't let her have the upper hand so I said I had somewhere to go.

For the last three months, my aunt had convinced me to let my guard down and filled my head with ideas about family always being there for me only to throw me out with no place to go. Being constantly hurt by people I loved when I needed them the most became draining. I was tired of everyone treating me like I owed them something after my mom passed away. More importantly, I was hurt that everyone saw what she was doing and no one spoke up for me because of my aunt's bipolar disorder. I felt like no one had my back that witnessed everything during entire trip. At that moment, I felt like disowning my dad's entire side of the family. The fear of people throwing my trials in my face was the

The Commandments of Womanhood

thing that made me fight my hardest battles alone and struggle in silence. During this trip, I felt one of my worst fears come to haunt me.

My cousin began texting me, letting me know she had my back, but she didn't want to get into it with her mother. She said my feelings were valid, but all I could think was why didn't anyone call her out if that were true. I loved her so much, but the constant low blows when she's moody and under stress became too much for me. She told me I was hard to live with when I put my job in jeopardy every time I went over breaks helping with kids that were not mine. Ultimately I decided I didn't want to waste my paid time off being unhappy, so I chose to go back to Los Angeles. As I was waiting for my Uber with my bags outside, my older male cousin asked me why I was leaving and all I could do was close my eyes to keep from crying because I was so angry and tired of being hurt. I later found out that he assumed I rolled my eyes at him while ignoring him; I reached out to him after, only to not get a reply.

That night, I froze my butt off in the Chicago airport. I couldn't check in because I was 2 days early for my flight and I didn't have the extra money to buy an earlier flight. I asked a lady for a blanket and instead she upgraded my ticket so instead of waiting 48 hours at the airport I could go home on an early flight that left in a few hours. I misread my flight plan because I was tired and what I had mistaken for a 6 PM flight was actually a 6 AM flight. My day was slept away only to realize my error at 4pm and I panicked. I soon found my way on a flight that left at 9 PM, which I was grateful for. Homeless once again, I felt like I was running out of options. The need to find my own place was necessary because I was tired of being displaced.

    Before I got on the plane I called my old friend from middle school Domonique and she agreed to let me stay the night at her house. After getting lost in the terminal once arriving, I took an Uber to her house. We laid in her bed and I told about the stressful time I was having. The more I repeated the story, the more ridiculous my falling out with my aunty sounded. I couldn't figure out for the life of me why she continued to make me the target of her frustration.

The Commandments of Womanhood

The next day I went to my aunt's house and got the majority of my clothes. I booked a room for the weekend to clear my head. This was probably the cheapest and most low-budget establishment I ever stayed in. I was grateful for the rate that Hotwire was able to provide over the weekend last minute. It was one of those "Get this cheap rate, but you don't find out the hotel until you pay," deals.

Finally settling in, I took a much-needed hot shower after being in the airport for almost 21 hours. A few family members called and texted me. I called my older cousin Jamila back after she'd called me twice. We had the longest conversation we ever had in my life. She tried to get me to understand the severity of her mother's bipolar mental health. In my true stubborn fashion, I let her know I understood, but I was tired of our family making excuses for my aunt's actions. We always made it a priority to conform around her mood swings and make excuses for her actions. We shared so much in that conversation and for the next four weeks my older cousin became such a big help to me.

The Commandments of Womanhood

Jamila taught me so many lessons and let me know that just because one person hurts me, I can't make that my excuse to feel like that about everybody. About a month prior to these events, one of my dad's nephews reached out to me and I gave him the cold shoulder because I didn't want to meet anymore of my dad's family. I felt like it was too late for me to want their acceptance because I felt like besides my aunt and her children, no one ever tried to be in my life.

I had an uncle who lived closer than my aunt and I can count on one hand the times I'd seen him growing up. I hope to one day be able to speak with my cousin who I turned away and apologize because that was not me. It was the broken, guarded shell of the person I was at the time. I will forever be grateful to my cousin Jamila for the talks we had and her taking me apartment hunting. The talks we had meant more to me than she will ever know. During this time, she also convinced me to go back to my aunt's house while she was still in Illinois and stack up rather than staying at hotels.

I went to church consistently and tithed obediently. One Sunday after church I walked up to my

The Commandments of Womanhood

pastor and asked him if he could pray for me. I can't explain it, but you can feel the Holy Spirit surrounding him. The next thing I knew tears were streaming down my face. My pastor asked me if I was okay and for the first time in my life I admitted that I wasn't. He told me to come meet with him that week and I was so nervous. The funny thing is about a week prior I had decided to try therapy and I searched free groups online only to come up with dead ends. I had been going to my church for around 4 years and I'd never really said much to my pastor, but something always told me I should. I desperately wanted to be more involved in ministry, but it seemed like every time my schedule would prevent me from doing so.

    I rushed and took off early to get to our session. My pastor arrived behind schedule, which didn't matter to me because I was trying to brace myself for this meeting. Later on I learned my pastor was having a rough week and still managed to make it a priority to meet with me. Another member of our church sat in the session with us named Danny. I'd seen him around before, but I'd never met him formally. My session was unlike what I imagined. In my head he was going to tell me what I needed to do with my life and give me clarity on my purpose, but it was very different. Instead of being lectured, my pastor let me vent and it was something I needed to do. I let a lot of things off my chest, but I didn't say everything. It was amazing to release things so openly and he let me know that his office was a safe place.

Pastor Michael Fisher let me know that my feelings were valid and I wasn't alone. Instead of forming his own opinions, he listened to me and prayed that God would bring people into my life that were genuine. He prayed for people I could feel safe with completely without feeling like I had to watch my back or owe them anything. That session will forever hold a place in my heart.

A couple of weeks passed and I still wasn't able to find an apartment. I was looking for anyone to give me a chance. I even went to the valley in an Uber and walked around on foot while my back ached with no luck. Eventually it was time for my aunt to return and the promise of reconciliation seemed like it wasn't going to

The Commandments of Womanhood

happen since she was still mad at me. I called my friend/ex coworker Lakeisha and asked her if I could stay with her for two weeks until I found a place. She opened up her home to me unlike any other person before. She never made me feel like a burden although sometimes she did give me anxiety because she worried a lot, but who could blame her she had her entire family's issues on her back. I would offer to give her money and she would always refuse. Even the sweetest people I had met in my life never declined money when offered so it was weird to me that someone who I didn't know as long as many of closest friends would treat me as kindly as them.

  A week passed and I applied to places. There was still no word on any good news. I decided not to apply anymore to places until I heard from this upscale inexpensive studio I found. It was way smaller than what I'd been looking for, but I decided to settle. Focusing my intentions on this apartment, I claimed this to be mine. I learned another valuable lesson, which was: Don't get mad at God for not giving you what you didn't ask for. I had been looking for almost 8 months and filling out so many applications to places that I'd simply settled on. When we settle and forget God's promise, we doubt the miracles that he can work out on our behalf. My apartment could've been mine sooner, but I kept getting scared of the unknown instead of taking a full leap of faith.

It was going on my second week and I knew I had to stick to my timeline to move out because my friend's sister was coming the day after I left. There were only three days to spare before I would be forced to go to a shelter and possibly quit my job. In order to work from home, my job required a proper workspace and hard wired internet, so I felt like I was running out of options. It seemed like there was no way out of this mess. I was praying and going to church, but I started to feel like God had abandoned me. We have to learn not to mistake God's silence or delay for a no because sometimes His delayed breakthrough is simply a "not yet."

There were a few potential places like a roommate situation I found on Craigslist and a sublease for three weeks to help a girl not break her lease, but it was those exact experiences in the past that brought me

The Commandments of Womanhood

to the place of having no options. None of the options I found made me feel secure, and this time I wanted things to be different. Hopping on the next opportunity just because it seemed to be good enough could longer be my option. This next season that God was taking me through required complete trust in Him and no back up plan.

    Security was what I desperately wanted. This place had to be for me, in my name, and not borrowed. Worrying about how many people had put in applications before mine couldn't matter. The negative thoughts started to eat at my faith and I started to question if God was still even working on my behalf. In this moment I began to pray and ask God to work something out for me. Transparently, I told him my faith was dwindling and I needed a miracle to be worked out on my behalf. I told God if he could raise Jesus on the 3rd day, then surely an apartment would be nothing for him. With humble gratitude, I began to thank him for the roof that was currently over my head. I told God I wanted him to work a miracle so big that I would never want to question Him again.

The Commandments of Womanhood

    I didn't really focus on putting too much thought into applying anymore. Eventually, I had found out that I didn't get the studio apartment that I applied to. Still remaining hopeful, I just knew that my apartment would find me. This was my mindset in the beginning and somehow I lost that frame of mind when it started getting close to the wire. A girl messaged me about renting a room in a two bedroom with her and her significant other. I set up a time knowing good and well that's not what I wanted. An hour before going to view the unit, I didn't have the will to go so I told her I'd reschedule for Sunday.

    At 7:30 PM, I got a random email from a Craigslist post asking me if I wanted to view a 1-bedroom unit that night. I thought it was odd to have an open house that late, but it felt right so I said absolutely and began getting ready. Instead of having to take an Uber, my friend offered to come home and drive me. I arrived and was greeted by a handsome man. He was very friendly and I viewed the unit amazed. It had everything I desired; hardwood floors, granite

The Commandments of Womanhood

countertops, and a nice up to date kitchen. I was sold to say the least.

He told me what was required for the unit. I was pleasantly surprised on how low the requirements for this place was in comparison to the ones I viewed prior, because it matched exactly what I wanted to the last detail. I asked him how long was the application process and he told me that he could let me know how it was looking as soon as I applied. I had to pinch myself to keep from feeling like I was dreaming. He gave me all the details and I applied as soon as I went back to my friend's apartment. I applied and like he said, he was giving me feedback as soon as I finished the application. I sent him references and a letter of recommendation.

My apartment literally found me; I applied, got approved and moved in within less than 24 hours from viewing the unit. I wasn't supposed to get paid until Monday, but randomly I got paid on Saturday, which never happens. God worked it out to where I had more than enough money to cover my first month and deposit. My cousin's best friend Sierra even offered to help me

The Commandments of Womanhood

move without me asking or even giving her anything in return.

    If you don't know anything else, realize that God is the plug and the foundation of any blessing. 100 percent of our problems He can resolve if we simply trust in Him. God allowed me to walk into this blessing without having even having a California ID. Me losing my ID in an Uber was the main reason I couldn't go back to a hotel. God literally took away every back up plan I had until I realized that with Him no back up plan is necessary. I appreciate everyone who added to my evolution whether the experience was pleasant or not. I've learned to find the blessing and the lesson in every struggle I've encountered. It is through God that I am even all that am.

    Never trust man more than you trust in God's promise. When I gave my situation to the Lord He did amazing things. I spent 8 months homeless because I refused to fully put all my trust in the Lord rather than people. He took me out of my comfort zone in order to come to Him with my problems. I was prideful and I would have rather struggled than ever admit when I

The Commandments of Womanhood

needed help. He taught me never to get comfortable within a job, friendship, or even an apartment that wasn't in my name. Everything is temporary so the struggle you think you're going through is really a blessing that's working on your behalf. In the first few days that I stayed at my new apartment, I found healing. There was comfort in the silence and so much gratitude sleeping on the $20 air mattress I purchased from Walgreens while waiting for my bed to be delivered from storage. Each day I cried in wonder as I noticed how perfect my apartment was.

    The more I really looked around, the more I realized the small things that matched my wants to a T. You never realize something as small as having a toilet with buttons instead of a handle until there are times that you remember not having a working toilet that flushed. There was gratitude in having an up to date clean shower because there was a time when I had to shower while standing in two feet of clogged dirty water. I began to get so overwhelmed with gratitude by even the smallest things within my new apartment. I completely trusted

The Commandments of Womanhood

God and noticed each blessing He began to do in my life and I began to hear His voice again.

Always carrying so many bags often made me sad that I was there for so many people yet no one could offer a helping hand to lighten my load. I had no safety net to depend on, but I was the driving force and security for so many around me. We have to stop waiting for others to inspire us, and start inspiring ourselves. *Some trials require us to overcome alone in order to learn the bigger lesson. Everyone can't help you fight your bondage and it's not their responsibility to do so.* The moment I acknowledged my giving spirit and let go of resentment towards others for not reciprocating that to me, I was able to become free of my own afflictions. Sometimes the wonderful things about you are not so easily reciprocated because it may be your gift. You can't worry about why people are the way they are. You have to obtain the ability to let go of those bags that weigh so heavily on you. Don't let the baggage you carry hinder your progression and evolution.

We as women do not have to harden ourselves and try to be strong in every situation. The society we

The Commandments of Womanhood

live in has forced us to do so, but we should remember there is strength in sensitivity. You should allow yourself to digest in a way that gives you the ability to move past and elevate. *There is strength in connecting with your emotions because that means you are aware. To become aware is to acknowledge. When you acknowledge you absorb and connect.*

    As women, we try so hard to have it all together. It is okay not to always have it together or know the answers to the unknown. However, if you choose positivity and happiness without dwelling in the darkness, you will be able to get through anything and climb the highest mountains. The easiest way to become happy, as far-fetched as it sounds, is to simply be happy—so start now. Let happiness consume you so much so that you overflow with love; and if you don't know what love is, remember God is Love

The Commandments of Womanhood

The Commandments of Womanhood

Your Body is a Temple

ACT LIKE IT

Rewind back to the tender age of 22—*The Artist* was still somewhat in the picture, but irrelevant enough not to be a major factor when it came to losing my virginity. After so many steamy yet failed attempts with him, I pretty much got the hint that he wasn't supposed to be my first. He was just someone to focus on in the meantime. During this time, I was going out a lot with my friend and I could never seem to find anyone worthwhile that I wanted to talk to. I was tired of getting to know guys only for them to dub themselves unworthy of me once they found out I was a virgin.

One time while out with my friend, I met this handsome guy who was a film student at Pepperdine University. We sat for hours in a lobby talking and he seemed to read my soul. He asked me about past relationships and was surprised to hear there were none.

The Commandments of Womanhood

The more we began talking, the more he opened up my mind as to why I was single. He told me I had a guard up that reflected as a repellent and that guard stopped me from finding love. He seemed nice and I'll always remember the conversation we had. At the time I felt like he was another jerk brushing me off since after meeting we never really talked again. We had so much chemistry, but I realize that *Pepperdine* was just a messenger from God sent to give me enlightenment.

There was a guy at work that I really liked. He used to train me at the gym and give me rides home from work. *J* sent me so many mixed signals, but he never made a direct move on me. Everyone at our job saw the chemistry, but we never dated or anything. *J* was genuinely nice to me, and as much he flirted I couldn't understand why nothing ever went further romantically.

After *J* ended up transferring to a different location, and I got moved to a new location, I was finally over the expectation of running into Mr. Right and I was done being open to finding love. I decided I just wanted to have fun. This was a time where I was just searching for some type of release, but I didn't even know what I

The Commandments of Womanhood

was chasing. Eventually I met the *Scorpio*. I'd never talked to a guy who looked like him. He was different than the usual pretty boys that I talked to. We talked briefly and he seemed cool, but I knew this would be strictly a sexual thing. There was nothing deep as far as getting to know each on an intellectual level. I didn't want to get to know him, so I began to sexualize him in a sense. We made plans for him to come over soon.

When he came over I made sure I smelt good, got a cute lace bra and panty set, and was drunk enough to build up the courage to go through with going all the way. There wasn't really much small talk when he came over to my apartment. He took the lead, making the first move after awkward forced conversation, and several hours later I was no longer a virgin.

They say that women become attached to their firsts, but I wasn't, and many of my friends weren't either. We were strangers and that's how I wanted it to be. My first time was very uncomfortable and there was literally no chemistry. Once the temporary high of losing my virginity wore off, I kept thinking back to all the signs with different people that I ignored in the past. A

The Commandments of Womanhood

week prior to losing my virginity my friend told me that she caught herpes from getting oral and before that there were several times with *The Artist* where there were clear warnings telling me to wait. Waiting just seemed impossible after being the only single friend all my life.

    After my first time, I tried to end things with the *Scorpio*. Once he found out he took my virginity, he was obsessed with proving he could satisfy me. After we talked about our first night together, I admitted that I didn't reach a climax so he wanted to redeem himself I guess. We hooked up once more after my first time only for me to get annoyed and disappointed with yet another failed experience. Before getting in the shower, I sent him a text to let himself out and delete my number. Sex was so pointless, and I began wondering why I'd been in such a rush to lose it to begin with. There were so many signs for me to hold on to my gift and I gave it away to a stranger only to feel nothing. All I felt was emptiness and there was no enjoyment on my part.

    After four failed and unfulfilling attempts at having sex, I learned why God intended this sacred act for married couples. More than the sex itself, there is

The Commandments of Womanhood

intimacy on a different level and I never allowed myself to be vulnerable enough with anyone to feel an intimate connection. Less than two months sexually active made me realize that I couldn't find enjoyment in random hook-ups because my emotions were nonexistent. With this revelation, I started my walk with celibacy.

As time goes on in this day and age, we are no longer taught to respect our bodies as women. Maybe when you were younger, if you grew up in a household as religious as mine, you might've been taught to act like a lady or be modest. Respecting your body is not about simply being modest. How can you ever be a lady if you're never been taught the keys of success while experiencing your journey of womanhood?

Forget about every preconceived notion that has been embedded into your mind in regards to modesty. Respecting your body as a woman is about knowing your value and treating yourself accordingly. If you don't value yourself how can you expect anyone else to treat you with care and respect?

We have to raise our standards and stop settling for mediocrity. There is power in our bodies and with recognizing that, we should know this type of power is precious and shouldn't be taken for granted. The gift that we hold between our thighs is something that should be held on the highest pedestal. Some can probably attest that while sex can be enjoyable, it can be even more beautiful and profound when it's with a person that is deserving and in sync with your energy. You can be in a relationship and still not be in sync with your mate. Stop using a relationship status as the excuse for intimacy because it is more than that. This reality ties back into our previous discussion on protecting our energy. It is so important to find the value within and only share yourself with deserving people both physically and mentally. *You are not for everybody, so stop making yourself so available to anybody.*

Forget about what society says with its double standards of sexuality. It doesn't matter how late you learn this lesson of self-value. It is never too late to start valuing your body and raising your standards. By making the conscious decision not to think hasty just because emotions are high and temptation is near, you are taking the first step to raising your standard of self-

The Commandments of Womanhood

worth. You are a Woman, one of God's greatest creations, and your body should hold exclusivity.

This chapter was not created to shame women in regards to promiscuity, but to remind of us of how precious we are. You can be liberated within your body without giving it away to undeserving people. This is about making more conscious and well-thought out decisions to whom you share the most sacred parts of yourself with. You always have a choice no matter what your mileage may have been in the past. Don't let anybody try to convince you otherwise. You are not worthless and your past decisions do not control the new mindset you have the ability to develop.

When sharing your body with another person you should always keep in mind numerous key points: Is this person's energy balanced? Does this person respect my body? Is this person currently suffering deep-rooted afflictions? Do we share the same values or morals? Does this person have baggage that I am willing to carry? These factors are very important and if you have an unpleasant answer when you ask yourself any of these questions regarding the person you are thinking about

The Commandments of Womanhood

being intimate with, then that should be a clear indicator of what your next action should be. You will find that most of the questions can only be answered with pleasantry when concerning your spouse, because when you marry someone you are marrying all of them. This is the exact reason why we should wait until marriage. We as women have to lead our examples down to our children in order to create a new, mindful generation.

The amount of single mothers has skyrocketed tremendously throughout the decades. This portion is in no way intended to throw shade at women who are single and unwed, but merely to share enlightenment from experience and observation. We deserve more than being alone to raise our offspring, and our children deserve more than a one-parent household, because reproduction between humans was not designed this way. As women we need to take responsibility for what we have contributed to some of this. I'm not referring to victims of rape or women who have lost the fathers of their children to death, I'm referring to those of us who have children with men who don't respect us and who aren't present in our children's lives.

The Commandments of Womanhood

We live in a generation that is so overly obsessed with relationship goals that we fail to get to know the person we create life with. This is the time where there are more divorces and single parent households than marriages. Although we don't have control over another person's actions, we must also learn to be better judges of character. We can feel deeply for another person yet choose not to tolerate their character. It takes strength and courage not give into temporary emotions for quick pleasure.

Even if we don't admit it to ourselves aloud, I can guarantee that many of our results of single motherhood would have turned out differently had we taken a moment to ask ourselves more important questions before intimacy. Stop giving into intimacy out of convenience and comfort. Sometimes we continue to stay and give ourselves to undeserving people because it's familiar and all we've known. The familiar begins to taunt us of lies that we can't do better. Don't be mistaken, because you can do better and you deserve better.

The Commandments of Womanhood

Time as well as close observations reveal all. The wolf in sheep's clothing would've inevitably shown its true colors had we been more aware and mindful of the signs that were in front of us. The person you conceived your child with was who they were before the child was born, thought of, or created. Sometimes we choose to ignore the signs because we are too blinded by temporary emotions and temptation. We must continue to be aware in our actions and handle ourselves accordingly.

Don't let emotions cloud your judgment. Some may say it's easier said than done, but it takes discipline as well as a strong mind to execute this. We are strong enough to discipline our minds to make better decisions. As women we are allowed to be selfish with our bodies and find power within it. We are deserving of someone who respects our bodies as much as we respect it. Make sure the person you choose to give your body to is worthy. Lust and attraction is not enough. You have to know without any doubt that this person is worth all of you. Any doubt about your partner should be the answer that helps you make the conscious decision not to

The Commandments of Womanhood

become intimate with that person. Take your time and get to know a person. I spent so much time rushing nature and feeling uneasy when anyone took too long to approach me that I was not realizing I wasn't whole myself. If I would've met my soul mate during the times I claimed I was open to finding him, he would've passed me by because I wasn't ready. I didn't even know my purpose, so what would I have done with my soul mate.

Out of all my friends I was the last one who started having sex. I had a fear of intimacy because that would show me in a vulnerable state. For a while, I found comfort in my virginity because it was easier for me to be hard and tough. It was easier not to show emotion and let my guard down. Being closed off was simple, and subconsciously I was running from myself. I do not regret the three partners I've had. However, knowing what I know now, I could've waited and valued myself far more than settling for a temporary illusion. Sex is everywhere you turn in media and it's so easy to get lost in the sauce. I lost hope that I'd ever be in a relationship or be married because I'd never dated before so I decided to settle for fun buddies. It wasn't fun, but merely meaningless sex with undeserving people because I failed to see that God was still building and perfecting my husband. Sex is about 70% mental more than anything, and if you are as emotionally detached as I used to be, sex can feel as meaningless as bumping into a dresser. It took me having sex four times to realize that a detached soul cannot fully connect with intimacy. My detached soul had to be healed.

When we learn to overcome our bondage we will begin to experience things greater than our wildest dreams. I could never get full satisfaction because I was never emotionally invested. Celibacy became a path that I chose because I realized that I was worth more than giving myself freely to people who were unworthy. Sure there is temporary sensations and satisfaction, but without your mind being an acting participant that simply means nothing.

Even if you're in a relationship already with someone and you've had premarital sex in the past, it's never too late to begin practicing the wait. I had a friend who became celibate after she had lost her virginity with her boyfriend. They were active for a while, and the

The Commandments of Womanhood

more that they grew within ministry she realized that she didn't want to keep unapologetically sinning instead of growing within God's word. Her and her boyfriend began to find hobbies that they enjoyed together like cooking and working out. Eventually, years later, they got married, but this all goes to say that it's never too late to begin the wait. Relationship or not, you can begin whenever. Our God is a forgiving Father and He knows everything about us, so don't let your past make you ashamed or feel like you can't become celibate or decide to wait until marriage.

Sex should not be used as an escape from your reality or a coping mechanism like it normally is for so many women. As women, we deserve for it to mean more. We deserve more than one-night stands and temporary satisfactions. You should feel special enough that not just can anyone experience your enchanted garden. We can try all we want to develop a "player" mentality, but at the end of the day we are only playing ourselves.

After you wake up from the hurt and pain, realize that you can never unsex whom you gave yourself to.

The Commandments of Womanhood

You can choose to be different, but everything happens for a reason. Regardless of if you've had 3 partners or 40, you can choose to love yourself enough to become selective. I don't believe in the double standards of promiscuity within genders. Both men and women should love themselves enough to maintain exclusivity within their bodies. *Everyone should not be welcomed into your home, for that opens up the opportunity for people to leave behind unwanted items as well as take things without returning them.* Our body is our home while living on earth, so why not be mindful of who we invite into our space. As women, we should be conscious and mindful of the value within our kingdom.

The Commandments of Womanhood

The Commandments of Womanhood

Seek No Validation

Often, more times than not, we as women tend to forget we are not validated parking. Stop waiting for another person to validate your existence. You don't need anyone to tell you that you're good enough. This is a known fact, and once you realize this you will have the ability to soar higher than a skyscraper. We often fail to realize the power within ourselves. The moment we stop looking for another to boost our confidence, the happier we'll become. People can have the habit of hurting you when you open yourself up to their negative, demeaning energy. *Allowing another person to belittle and demean you is an act of violence against yourself.* You have a choice to remove yourself from the mental attacks that others try to cause.

You are enough, and everything you do is enough. Stop looking to others to save you from yourself. The power has always been within you. You hold the key to your own happiness and success. As

The Commandments of Womanhood

women we fail to realize how much power we hold within ourselves. Why are we so afraid to be great? Doubt from another individual should be irrelevant. Turn the voices off. Shut off the hate and gravitate towards a place of self-assurance. Don't give other people the power to defeat you.

    The other day I learned a great lesson as I was walking to the bank. I was speed-walking so fast that I didn't notice I dropped my paycheck out of my pocket. All the obstacles I had to go through in order to pick this up, only to carelessly forget it on the sidewalk. I was nearly at the entrance of the building when I reach into my pocket and realize my check was not there. I immediately began to panic and wanted to scream—wait actually, I did scream. I screamed very loudly. Here I am in Santa Monica screaming like a madwoman in the middle of the sidewalk. Not only was I missing money at work by going out of my way to get a check that was supposed to be directly deposited into my account, I had no room to waste any money because this was when I found out I was losing my apartment. I had to check myself quickly and realize I was better than overreacting.

The Commandments of Womanhood

I silently told myself nobody picked it up and it was there on the sidewalk. "Nobody picked it up and it's going to be there on the sidewalk," I chanted silently. As I walked several blocks down the street passing a homeless man rolling around in the dirt, I noticed my check neatly folded in the middle of the sidewalk.

The moment I saw this was the moment I truly knew that this book was detrimental to the young women of my generation and I couldn't just leave them behind to bask in the mindset caused by the mud our society has thrown on us. As urgent as I had to walk back to pick up my check off the sidewalk, I feel the same urgency picking up the young women of my generation because we are so important. You are so valuable yet you are left on the sidewalk and nobody took the time to pick you up. Nobody took the time to teach many of you how to value yourself, so you seek constant validation from others as if you're a car.

We tend to seek validation in our significant others as well as our friends and family. The people who tend to be the closest to us have knocked us down on the sidewalk. Here we are rolling in the mud thinking our

The Commandments of Womanhood

scars define us. What a shame it is not to know our own worth with the constant ridicule from others knocking down our dreams and self-esteem.

We must start treating ourselves like newborn babies in everything we do. Just like we would not want people contaminating our infant with their germs because the baby's immune system isn't strong enough, we need to use that same mentality to protect our spirit. We must protect our dreams, hearts, and minds. Such power should be handled with delicacy and care. Give yourself something to be proud of. Don't wait for another person to praise you. Motivate and encourage yourself, for you are a queen and should tolerate nothing less than the highest accolades. You are in a category of your own and not everyone will be able to relate. People hate what they do not understand. Figure out what your purpose is and become it. Stop trying to conform to what others want you to become and be yourself. Be the powerful woman God has destined you to become.

Your greatness is a threat, so what better way to stagnate your greatness than to tear down your confidence. What better way to stop you from loving

The Commandments of Womanhood

yourself than to crush your spirit? It's not what people call you, but what you answer to; and from this moment on you should only answer to Queen because that is what you are. You are neither a peasant nor a stepstool. Rise up Queen, stand proud, and never give another person the opportunity to knock you down.

The Commandments of Womanhood

The Commandments of Womanhood

Thou Shalt Not Settle for Inconsistency

Inconsistent behavior is one that has been taught from a very early age. Maybe one of your parents was never around, or a loved one had the horrible habit of dropping back into your life whenever they felt like it. Not only do they introduce you to their inconsistent nature, they also pick and choose the times in which they want to be the person you need them to be. People you care about tend to have a way of making you feel as though you are only worthy of unrequited love and inconsistency, but the truth is your worth so much more.

While being brainwashed, many of us have slowly conditioned our minds to believe that these actions are acceptable. It is not acceptable and we have to know that this is not something that should be taken lightly. You should be a priority because you are worthy

The Commandments of Womanhood

of so much more than being reduced to a backup plan, option, or last resort.

The worst thing anybody can do is waste your time. Time wasted is something you can never get back, and a person who constantly wastes your time is disrespectful. If someone does not value something as important as your time, that is a clear indication that they do not respect you. To play with something as valuable as time is to undermine your very existence. Time is something that is not promised and while we often calculate it as though there is an unlimited supply of it, this is something that is very limited in our lives. One of the only things a person really has to give another is their word and once that is broken, trust becomes a thing of the past.

The Artist was very inconsistent and what irritated me about his actions is that he didn't realize his error. You might look at me and wonder how did I get played by a man who wasn't even sure if he was into women? I often asked myself how did I protect myself and still end up the fool? Simply said, I played myself. I didn't trust in the Lord to bring me the mate I deserved. I had a bad habit calling *the Artist* when I was feeling low and forgetting my worth. Even after writing the first version of this book, I thought I was done with him because I had this new mindset.

After I wrote the first version of this book I was so sure of myself. I initially reached back out to be his friend and get closure because I did value the conversations we had in the past. Us being so alike often clouded my judgment and made me sometimes wonder about what would happen if I did give him a real chance. Ultimately I had to realize is that we were not soul mates and there wasn't a happily ever after in my future that included him. I had to stop seeking out closure because it always led to my progress going backwards. Our inner demons just knew each other and the devil has a way of coming in all forms especially those hidden insecurities. I made him feel better, yet he continued to make my wounds deeper without my permission, and subconsciously I allowed him to do this.

Soul ties are real and we were both addicted to masturbation as well as pornography. For me, my addiction to masturbation began at 3 when a molested

The Commandments of Womanhood

family member taught one of cousins how people touch themselves; they then showed me, and that sensation became my medication. It made me feel free, and unlike the few times I had sex, I actually enjoyed it.

 Eventually after I talked to him again, I realized that he was turning me into the exact opposite type of woman that I was trying to become. How could I minister or even inspire anyone while still messing with a man who didn't respect my time? I felt worthless sneaking in his grandmother's house in the middle of the night, especially because I'd always had my own place during the time we talked prior. He eventually stopped texting me, and it infuriated me because I tried everything with him. I tried being understanding, I tried being his friend, I tried not caring, and then eventually found myself caring in the end.

 He liked the idea of building with a woman like me without becoming the man I hoped for him to become. I was supportive to his dreams and I inspired him regardless of how angry he made me. Still to this day I only want to see him win, but I realize he's no good for me; and as I've evolved I also realize he's not

The Commandments of Womanhood

good enough for me. The more time away from him the more I found myself realizing that I didn't even really know him. He showed me repeatedly who he really was, but I kept playing with fire as if I'd never get burned.

    I deserve a man who sees more than late night make out sessions tiptoeing in his grandmother's house. I deserve a man that knows what and who he wants. I deserve a man of God, not a lost boy full of excuses with no real ambition. That was another reason I could never bring myself to fall for him, because he was not a man of faith. I was too head over heels for the Lord not to be in a committed relationship with a man who loved God as much as me. I wanted a man who could give as much as he received, and an inconsistent boy in a man's body who couldn't make up his mind wouldn't cut it for me anymore. There was no more compromising sin to cover up my sin because it began to make me feel worse about myself.

    I thank him for ignoring my texts in the end about a business endeavor and all the excuses he made in the past as to why he could never be honest with me. I was always honest with him and all he gave in return were

The Commandments of Womanhood

excuses. The only thing I ever asked of him was communication and all he gave was inconsistency.

Inconsistent behavior is so prevalent in our lives that we tend to make excuses for such intolerable acts. Maybe this person is busy or maybe they just forgot. Inconsistency is something that an excuse should never suffice for. A person will always make time and create space for what is valuable to them. By tolerating such disrespectful behavior, we are granting too much power to another human being. It is not okay to be forgotten, because we are so valuable that we should always be remembered.

We are not fast food restaurants that stay open 24 hours. People cannot just come and go as they please. By allowing a person to continuously waste your time, you are not respecting yourself. Many will say inconsistency is not that deep, but it is, so much so that it had to become a commandment of womanhood. How dare we allow another person to disrespect us with such an act and then condition ourselves tolerate it? We should not make ourselves accustomed to these acts. You will only continue to attract the things that you allow and deem as acceptable. With this being said, we should have enough respect for others not to waste their time as well. To be consistent is to be accordant and compatible with another.

    Stop forcing compatibility out of comfort and if a person tells you who they are believe it the first time. We always hold on to hope that a person will change, but when will we realize that a man who repeatedly shows you he doesn't want to be tied down is the person they say they are? Maybe he tells you when you meet him that he's not looking for anything serious, but you stay and wonder why he's inconsistent. He told you before, but you ignored it because you wanted something that didn't exist in the first place. That wasn't the case for *the Artist* and I because he actually said he wanted something serious to start, but his actions proved different. Regardless of if they pull the wool over our eyes, listen to the signs the first time. Most of us hold out hope even when a person tells up front who they are and what they want. An inconsistent person should in no shape or form be included in your life for they are neither conducive nor compatible, irrespective of who

The Commandments of Womanhood

the person is. Take people for who they are and put them in the same category in which they put you. Stop making wishy-washy people a priority when you are only their back up plan.

We should not continue to hold space for people who do not respect us the way we should be respected. Observe, become aware, and then treat people accordingly. Do not inherit their disrespectful behavior, but become better than their actions. No longer make that person such a priority that they have the ability to disappoint you with their behavior. If we do not place all of our hope into the very human being that continues to hurt us, we will no longer be disappointed.

Be mindful to the games people play and don't allow such a person to puppeteer your emotions. We should always be aware and present enough not to allow such patterns. Tolerating such patterns is not conducive to your well-being. Subconsciously conditioning your mind to be okay with such behavior is another act of violence against yourself. Know what you want and never settle for anything less than the best.

The Commandments of Womanhood

The Commandments of Womanhood

Your Past Shall Not Define Your Future

"Though thy beginning was small, yet thy latter end should greatly increase. For enquire, I pray thee, of the former age, and prepare thyself to their fathers: (For we are but of yesterday, and know nothing, because our days upon earth are a shadow:)". Job 8:7-9

We always have a choice in the outcome of trials that occur in our life. Situations and heartache will inevitably arise, but we have to develop the strength to press forward and rise above the negativity that comes our way. How many times can we continue to use our circumstances as our excuse to fail? Your mother being a prostitute or not valuing and loving her body does not have to lead you down the same road of sexual promiscuity. Breaking the cycle of self-hate and abuse while creating a new story for yourself is possible.

The Commandments of Womanhood

Conditioning the mind after tragedy is difficult, but not impossible. Stop using your past as an excuse because you always have the ability to begin again. People often wonder how I find the strength to fight adversity when so much has happened to make me want to throw in the towel, and honestly I can say it was nothing but the grace of God. I should have been dead, but with God's strength and love I chose to press on. You have to believe that there is a divine purpose over your life because there is. Remove the mindset of doubt and know when a door closes another door with far greater rewards is waiting to open just for you.

Remain positive at all times regardless of what's going on around you. It's so hard to keep faith when so many things come at you daily, but it's possible. Mentally check yourself every time you feel discouraged and more importantly keep strong, like-minded people around you who can lift you up in order to get you back on track. Growing up I was never taught the commandments of womanhood. My mother was a great example of some key characteristics of a good woman, but she did not teach many lessons that I have learned. I

The Commandments of Womanhood

had to obtain this wisdom by living and observing the people around me. I had to see for myself the difference between wrong and right. I didn't get a chance to have the coming of age talks with my mom because she died when I was 15, leaving me an orphan. Even then, although we were close, I now see some pivotal lessons that were not taught nor executed by her.

I have endured a lot in my lifetime from nearly committing suicide a few times to being sexually assaulted by an older boy at a summer day camp. I've had my attacker try to drown me in a pool and I've been suffocated by a family member who would sit on me as well as stuff dirty socks in my mouth. I lost the majority of vision in my left eye the week after I graduated high school due to stress. There have been times when I had to miss meals for several days because I couldn't afford to eat and other times when I was homeless sleeping place to place. I've slept at a train station, and I've slept at a crappy hotel that gave me bug bites all over my body without even sleeping under the cover. There was a time when I had to endure living with both roaches and mice.

The Commandments of Womanhood

Through the grace of God, I was able to develop tough skin and not give up.

If you look up some of the most successful people of our time, more occasions than none, those people have been through some type of adversity in one way or another. We have conditioned ourselves to believe we have a high tolerance for pain in order to suppress our emotions. We all go through things and some have tougher trials than others. You always have two choices in life: to either let a situation affect you or channel your emotions and turn them into strength in order to fight for a better tomorrow. You have to believe in yourself to know that you can face anything.

We all have the keys to break the chains of the things that hold us bondage. Your parents not being present in your life can longer be used an excuse to fail. Somebody bullying or talking negatively about you is not an excuse to become a hateful soul. We have to find the strength, courage, and wisdom in every situation to reverse our bad situations into good ones. We have to break these cycles that have been passed down through generations. All we have is the choices and decisions that we choose to make in our lifetime.

The best motivation to becoming successful is our trials. No matter how heartbreaking and painful, these tests have the ability to become the right amount of fuel to elevate us beyond measure. You are whatever you tell yourself you are and it's just a matter of having enough discipline to make it true. It all starts with simply believing and having faith. With doing that, you also have to learn to have gratitude for the trials that have helped to shape your resilience.

There is strength in the pain we experience. Be precise and exact. Know what you want out of life and begin taking the action, because for every action there is a reaction. There is no such thing as failure. Failure is not reality, but just a made up excuse that was created to blind us from becoming the best versions of ourselves. The power within you is so great that it can build the most profound things if only you let it. You can win. You will win. You are a woman, and strength you shall become.

The Commandments of Womanhood

The Commandments of Womanhood

Finance Thyself with a Wealthy Mind

A woman is not a woman if she cannot provide for herself. Some say the wealthiest place in the world is the cemetery because there are so many people buried with greatness that was never tapped into. When you find your purpose, it will bring about everything that your heart truly desires. To whom much is given much is required, so we need to be prepared. We should be taught how to manage our money and experience an abundant quality of life.

This year I've read so many books about financial independence and prosperity by some remarkable self-made multi-millionaires. The overall message was the same. How can I not pass along my findings? Financial independence is very crucial with the advancement of women. Whether anyone has instilled this great tool in you or not, it's never too late to learn.

The Commandments of Womanhood

We always want to be a boss, but fail to inherit the mentality that helps make us into efficient ones. Incompetence and codependency are traits that we need to stay far away from. The number one thing that each self-made millionaire has taught me, and all seem to agree on, is the importance of saving and having a safety net.

All self-made millionaires share a common trait, which is the fact that they started with nothing; and with that being said, regardless of what your financial status is, you can always make a shift in your financial stability. Every time you make money it is extremely important to pay yourself first. By paying yourself first, I don't mean going on a shopping spree and buying everything your heart desires. Each time you get income, at least 10% of your income should be directly deposited into your savings account and in addition to that 10-15% percent of your yearly income should be used to enhance your intellect and growth as a successful being. Self-improvement is very important to being financially independent and we should always enhance our minds to become better.

The Commandments of Womanhood

Many will tell you your savings account should have enough money in it to live comfortably and pay your bills for at least 6 months minimum. That's just the beginning of savings, and I want you all to be better than a savings account that you constantly dabble into. Your savings account should ultimately become your money machine for years to come. Savings accounts with high interest rates are very important to have as well. The best way to save is if you don't see the money coming out in the first place. The mind can easily adapt when the money is not seen, so change your banking profile settings to hide your savings account. Don't cheat yourself; no matter how hard things get, continue to put the same consistent amount into your savings. When your income increases, so should the percentage of what you set aside for savings. Financial experts will tell you that the key to financial freedom is merely just saving, but more important than saving, one should learn the fundamentals of compounding.

It's not as complex as financial books try to make it out to be. Compounding is being able to have your money build without taking a loss. By compounding

The Commandments of Womanhood

your savings, you have the ability to grow your funds by more than 600% and set up a very wealthy life for your better tomorrow. If you can't start at 10%, start at 5 or 8 then gradually increase. You control the number. The most important thing is just to start and keep with it. We spend our whole lives being the worst investors by trading our time for money. We spend 8 hours of our day working for places that rob us of our time in exchange for money that can't even measure up to the time that we've lost. We must learn to work smarter and not harder.

  I have put together a 4 book reading guide to help you with achieving financial security and it goes as follows: The Science of Getting Rich by Wallace D Wattles, 365 Ways to Become a Millionaire by Brian Koslow, Million Dollar Money Saving Secrets by John C. McKibbon, and last but certainly not least Money, Master the Game: 7 Steps to Final Freedom by Tony Robbins. I put them in this particular order because of the way in which they enhance your mind. With each book your intellect grows more, until you are able to truly grasp the concept of achieving financial stability and security. We must build for our better tomorrows and enjoy living in the process, rather than trading our time without accumulating great memories to show for it.

Ultimately, you want to be able to reach a point where you create something so profound that you never have to physically work again and still manage to make money while you sleep. Work should be a choice not a chore. Imagine how much stress you can avoid by working because you want to and not because you have to. We must stop thinking small and allow ourselves to achieve everything our heart desires. There is enough wealth and abundance for everyone to become successful. The moment we lose the competitive mentality and stay in our lanes, things will begin to line up in order for us be taken to new heights.

One of the secrets to becoming wealthy is to provide a service that is lacking amongst many. By finding the lack within any field, you have the ability to create a need for your service. In addition to that, take the very talents you are good at and find a way to provide a helpful service to others while increasing your income substantially. Each year your income should increase, and eventually, we should apply that mindset to monthly as well as daily income.

Always look for ways to enhance your income and ability to create that income. Two people can work in the same field and one can become very wealthy while the other remains poor simply because of one small thing that they do. It's not because one person is smarter or better than the other, but the mindset that they choose to develop while pursuing their goals. Wealth is a mindset and you have to visualize everything that you want. After visualizing your wants meditate on them constantly until they are embedded in your mind and you begin taking the necessary action for every step you make can only bring you closer to your dreams. Eventually our actions will breathe life into the new ideas that help us attain the life we so desperately want.

The moment you begin taking these steps, you begin tapping into the creative part of your mind. The steps to success remain the same: Visualize the goal, believe you can achieve it, take the necessary actions to manifest that vision, and then receive it. In addition to

The Commandments of Womanhood

that, the most important thing is to be thankful for what you have in the meantime. You can't expect be blessed with more without being grateful for what you have at the present moment. Each step is equally important and they all have an important role in helping you achieve your goal.

The wealthiest people in the world became so by mastering the ability of taking very little risks to gain bigger rewards. We have this idea of being wealthy, but many of us lack the core tools to maintain the lifestyles we so desperately want. Jack Canfield, self-made millionaire and co-author of the Chicken Soup for the Soul series, always emphasizes the importance of being specific when planning your ideal life. We can say we want wealth and abundance, but without specifically outlining our ideal lifestyle and knowing the cost of our ideal lifestyle, we'll never know what we are working towards. Sometimes success and wealth from the outside looking in looks like it just happened overnight when in reality it was a series of small meticulous steps that caused a shift in the mindset to bring about bigger results.

The Commandments of Womanhood

Financial readiness should always be a priority. You have to feel it in order to become it, and figure out the steps to follow in order to manifest your dreams into reality. I am in no way, shape, or form a financial advisor, however, by applying even these basic tips that I've included in this brief chapter you can begin to shift some of your habits.

If you are in debt, the first step to becoming debt free is to stop focusing on debt. You are not debt; stop letting it consume you. If you continue to focus on debt and failure, you will only continue to attract more of it. If you begin focusing on wealth and prosperity, you will begin to attract more into your life. Set up automatic payments for your debt repayment so it comes out of your accounts each month. Don't get overwhelmed, just write everything down and make a plan to pay it off while focusing on things that can increase your income. Always keep track of everything you purchase.

We should be organized with our spending, as well as keep tabs on where our money is going. If you pay attention to things you carelessly spend a lot of your money on, you'll find that some things can be cut back on, which will leave you more money to invest in your better tomorrow. Making a budget is one of the best things you can do because it keeps spending under control and keeps you accountable for what you purchase. Whenever you go into a store, make sure you always have a list so you won't over spend because believe me it will come back to hurt you later.

While many people will tell you to take out multiple credit cards, I am here to tell you to be very mindful of taking out too many credit cards. You don't have to be afraid of credit cards, but you should always remember that they should solely be used in case of emergencies and not to cover the cost of things that are too far out of our budget. If you cannot afford to pay for something without it hurting afterwards, then you do not need to buy it. Most people have a bad habit of spending way more than they can afford, hence the reason why so many people ultimately go bankrupt. Spending carelessly without a safety net and plan in place is financial suicide. With a credit card you always want to use no more than 30% of the overall limit and always make your payments on time. On time payments can impact your credit score

The Commandments of Womanhood

in a big way. Even if you have to set an alarm on your phone, so be it, but make sure that your payments are made on time.

    Stop trying to keep up with the latest. I believe Tony Robbins said it best when he said we should stop being consumers and start being investors. Invest in your dream life. It is up to you to be prepared to handle yourself when financial hardships arise. It's better to have a plan, even when everything is going great, than to not have a plan at all. Live a life of abundance and not of gluttony, for one should never be greedy with wealth. As your wealth increases, remember to give back in some way. Tithing and giving back is important, and eventually you notice that you begin to walk into more doors due to being a cheerful giver. Always expect the unexpected. A woman who knows how to manage her money is a force to be reckoned with. It's always great to be spoiled, but at the end of the day we should know how to provide our own financial independence, because the only person who you have control over is yourself.

The Commandments of Womanhood

The Commandments of Womanhood

Become Thy Ideal Mate

In this day and age, there are so many requirements when looking for the perfect mate. We tend to have so many prerequisites without putting in nearly the same work on ourselves. Many would not even know what to do with their ideal mate if that person walked passed them. A girl will say she wants someone who respects her when she doesn't know the first thing about respecting herself. How can you want someone who takes pride in you when you present yourself to others in a manner that is utterly disrespectful to your own being?

You will always attract what you put out into the universe. If you want a person who is educated, you need to take the time to educate yourself and sharpen your own intellect. How can you want so much when all you do is simply bring coupons to the high-end buffet of your desires? If we have nothing of value within ourselves to offer another, then we should expect nothing more than the mediocrity that we are providing.

The Commandments of Womanhood

We can't expect someone to have it all together when we don't even have it together. The truth is we're all works in progress evolving day by day. Nobody is perfect and if we continue to search for this farfetched idea of perfection, we will be lonely forever. We should be able to build with our mates and help each other become the best we can be. Stop trying to match half-heartedly with 50/50, and start matching your partner 100 percent.

Us women must date ourselves first. Stop being serial daters hopping from relationship to relationship in search of validation and security. By continuing this pattern and mindset you will never attain what you seek. You can't skip the very first step: seeking what's within. We must learn to be whole within ourselves so that our mates compliment us not complete us. That's the problem with people today. So many of us are looking become complete with a person when God is the only one who can complete us. This reason alone is why there are so many unhappy couples that find themselves wanting more. If they were whole to begin with, the person that they attracted would've matched the person that they were.

In this day and age society tells us that if we are not entertaining another person constantly that we are lonely and unwanted; but we have to remember that our validation should begin and end only with ourselves. You don't need a relationship to be happy. I used to dream of happiness for my future life instead of trying to make myself happy during the now. You have to find happiness within yourself before being able to share that with anyone else. Get to know yourself and align yourself with what God has planned for you. Have you ever genuinely gotten to know you? When was the last time you took you somewhere nice and pampered yourself?

If you want someone who is spontaneous and keeps you on your toes, then you must first be adventurous alone. Date yourself and take yourself on an adventure. Travel and meet different people. Explore the wonders that God has placed on this earth. We have to learn how to become our ideal mate and fall in love with ourselves. It is possible to find and attract everything we

The Commandments of Womanhood

want in a mate, but you must first put out that same energy into the universe and become that, too. Learn yourself and become the best you that you can possibly be.

We can't continue to be lost souls creating destruction with other lost souls. Find comfort in being alone and becoming a better you. Love will happen in the midst of you living your purpose, so stop looking and let it find you. We live in the social media age, where everybody has somebody, or at least appear to. Even the strongest get lonely sometimes, but don't let that be the reason you settle for just anybody. It can take years, but it eventually weighs us down so much that we lose focus. Stop peeking! Stop looking at everyone else's garden and plant your own. Social media has a way of making even the strongest feel inadequate, so take a step back and focus on you. You never know the type of love you may stumble upon.

If you want someone respectful, then you must respect others as much as you respect yourself. We are whom we attract. *Birds of a feather flock together* is reality as a phrase. No matter how much you try to deny

The Commandments of Womanhood

it, in some shape or form you are connected and related in a way. Becoming your ideal mate is all about self-discovery. We need to become the very thing we want in another person. The principle always remains the same: Like attracts like. Become the best version of yourself, and you will attract a mate that with complements you. We must hold ourselves to the same standards that we set for another person.

To find someone trustworthy we have to be trusting and trustworthy ourselves. If we go looking for trouble within our happy home, we will only bring about the things that we so desperately seek to find. I used to have a coworker that was overly obsessed with keeping tabs on her boyfriend. She used to hack into his emails and would track his location with her phone. She'd constantly search for the worst in him not realizing that she was only creating and attracting negativity to her relationship. She even had her phone set up to where if he took screenshots of something it would automatically save to her phone. Every day she would go on his social media pages and search through the people who liked and commented on his posts.

The Commandments of Womanhood

So many women are obsessed with being detectives when it comes to their significant other that they fail to see the error of their ways and the negativity these ways attract toward their relationship. It's so easy to get so obsessed with a person to the point that you just want them all to yourself. But remember, you will always bring about what you think about most. By focusing and trying to find negativity, you will forever jinx your relationships whether romantic or simply platonic. What's done in the dark will always come to the light and by constantly seeking a bad situation that is exactly what you will receive. We've all obsessed over a person we care about, but we have to learn to look at our actions and tackle what is making us act that way. In most cases the reason we become so obsessed is because we don't fully know ourselves and we're insecure about something. When you know yourself fully, you learn that everything and everybody is temporary. If you stop being afraid to lose people you will stop being afraid to meet people. We should be secure enough in ourselves to stop seeking out the worst in others. Believe me, it's hard; but it takes time and self-evaluation.

The Commandments of Womanhood

The law of attraction is quite simple. If you want a person that makes you feel secure, you must eradicate the insecurity that you possess. You have to give the same things that you hope to receive. You can be in denial all you want about how you were the perfect person to someone and they did you wrong; but, is it actually true? It's a hard pill to swallow that our past actions have a major impact on things that we may encounter in the future. Nobody can honestly say that they have never done anything that has caused pain to another regardless if it was intentional or not. Everybody has caused pain in one way or the other. It was done and it will inevitably play a role in our lives, however, we have a choice on how big of an impact it can make in our present situations. Love yourself first and the rest will follow your lead.

The Commandments of Womanhood

The Commandments of Womanhood

Always Remember Thy Royalty

So easily we forget who we are throughout the trials and tribulations of this thing we call life. Women are a gift from the Most-High, and we should always remember who we are. We are the Goddesses of the earth. We are imperfectly perfect in divine creation sent to this world to birth the nation. It is important that we never lose ourselves nor forget our worth.

I spent more than half my life consumed by suicidal thoughts and I self-sabotaged myself on a daily. What I've come to realize is that the time you are the unhappiest is when you don't know your purpose and aren't living that purpose in some way. Living without purpose makes you feel lost and inadequate, like you're not doing enough. Life has a way of getting us off track so much that we begin to forget who we are. I urge my generation, and the generations to come, to bring things back to reality and start living in the now again. Stop

The Commandments of Womanhood

flexing for outsiders and start living for real. I never knew love until I began to love myself with the help of God's love. Growing up not having much family or people in your corner, you begin to feel like your life is insignificant. There were many days when I felt my life was worthless. I didn't have parents or grandparents; I wasn't in love like most of my friends; I didn't have many friends to even begin with; and I isolated myself. I didn't know what I was living for, and I felt incredibly alone.

In high school, I developed a defense mechanism that came in the form of my love for photography. It was a way I could create without being in the spotlight. I'd rather hide behind a lens than get in front of it. All my life people were drawn to me and I rebelled against it. I put so much time, effort, and money into my photography never getting anywhere other than one plateau after the next. I even started designing clothes. I didn't get the recognition I felt I deserved—not because I didn't do it well, but because I was living some else's purpose instead of my own.

The Commandments of Womanhood

Do what you love. Happiness isn't equated to money, status, or people around you. Granted those things can be around during your rise to happiness, but it's more about God than anyone else. Be real with yourself; don't do what you had to convince yourself you like. Do what consumes you with the most magnificent joy, even if it's what you think is the smallest of tasks. Everybody has a different purpose but they're all equally important.

Continue to live within that joy and watch how that begins to manifest a change throughout your entire life. Trials come in order to refocus us and set us back on track to what we are supposed to do. We get too comfortable in mediocrity, so life pulls us back on our path by making us uncomfortable in our current circumstance. That's when we then begin to go to different levels. Out of everything that was considered bad to happen to me, I can honestly say that nothing worked against me. Even the most painful of events have shaped me into a better person and made me stronger.

A pastor that I used to respect and look up to very much told a class during a business-branding workshop

The Commandments of Womanhood

that everyone has a story and nobody wants to hear yours. The truth is that my story is very important and so is each person reading this book's, in addition every other person in the world's. No matter how big or small, your story is important. Your struggle is important. I believe if more people shared their stories we could actually build a better foundation for growth and inspire each other. During this small workshop, I felt out of place trying to share my big realities with small-minded people. You have to be careful with whom you share your destiny because some people have the ability to kill your dreams if you're not convinced of your purpose. People don't do it maliciously, but sometimes your purpose might be too great for others to comprehend.

    I told this same pastor during the seminar that I wanted to eventually have 7-8 successful businesses, but the first step was this book. He thought he was being helpful and honest by telling me that people who have 7 or 8 businesses at once aren't successful. I don't fault him for his comment because that's how the world has conditioned us to think. There are so many multi-billionaires that have several business and multiple

The Commandments of Womanhood

streams of income. All of their businesses are connected in one way or another, but the thing that successful people get right is the fact that naysayers have no power to kill their mindset. Sometimes a small-minded person can't comprehend your big destiny, and that is okay. They aren't meant to because you can show them better than you can tell them. You literally can do anything you set your mind to because the possibilities are endless. Just think, if my mom listened to the pastor who told her she was too overweight to carry a child I wouldn't be here to help so many women who needed to read this book.

    I wish I had a me that I am now when I was younger to remind me of all these things that I somehow forgot. The world is a cruel place and as we begin to grow older, we start to notice the negativity around us. That negativity begins to throw us off track. We are shown so many negative images that it begins to play on our conscience. When those insidious thoughts try to overpower you, learn to focus on what's bigger than you. Not knowing your purpose can lead you down a dark road if you let it; and once you realize how life works,

The Commandments of Womanhood

you begin to find a new appreciation for everything around you.

    We are worthy of unconditional love. We are worthy of respect. We are worthy of happiness. We are worthy of everything good and pure. We are the inhabitants of our own inhibitions and have the ability to attain the desires of our hearts. We have control over our lives regardless of the situations that have tried to make us believe otherwise. Protecting our energy, mind, body, and spirit is vital to our progression. Don't let society's views determine the type person you choose to become. We can break the chains of bondage. We are Women. We are Queens. We are gifts from God.

The Commandments of Womanhood

The Commandments of Womanhood

Lost Queen

You think by bringing him into your bedroom
you can teach him how to love you.
Thinking he really loves you when all he wants to do is sex
you, caress you, undress you.

Those eyes filled to the brim with lust yet you constantly
confuse it with love. He doesn't value your body, but
you've convinced it to your mind. He's tainted all of your
energy, but queen you're just too blind to see. Simply
setting yourself up for misery because you're so afraid of
being lonely.

Falling fast for temporary lovers to compensate for the
love you've never been shown from your mother. Lovin oh
so deep yet you weep as you sleep. Oblivious to the self-
love within you that's been misconstrued because you've
never known the truth.

You think you truly love yourself, but you constantly
destroy yourself. You continuously avoid yourself. It's so

The Commandments of Womanhood

easy to let the demons inside use you, fool you, abuse you. Acts of violence committed daily against you by you because you're okay with being sexualized and nourishing your beautiful soul with lies.

Accumulating the numerous soul ties from all the men you've let between your thighs. It's never too late to elevate yourself because you are worthy. You are worthy of the highest praise and accolades.

Baby girl, did you know you were a queen?

Mama never showed you and daddy never told you. Eradicate the old you and stop letting those deep-rooted scars control you. Don't let them demons continue to mold you and hold you- captive.

Hey Queen, did you know you can have anything?

You can have anything your heart desires instead of surrounding yourself by habitual liars. Your intentions are

The Commandments of Womanhood

so pure, but you let those many erections be your cure. Logic so obscure once your panties hit the floor.

Rise up Queen, remember who you are. Don't let this world convince you to ever dim that star.

The Commandments of Womanhood

The Commandments of Womanhood

Epilogue

Like Water

"Moving down the streams of my lifetime
Pulls the fascination in my sleeve
Cooling off the fire of my longing
Boiling off my cold within his heat
Melting down the walls of inhibition
Evaporating all of my fears
Baptizing me into complete submission
Dissolving my condition with his tears
He's just like the water
I ain't felt this way in years"

Lauryn Hill

This book began as frustration for the way I saw our generation headed and it turned into a love letter to Womanhood. There were times writing this book when I felt like it wasn't even myself talking. I read this book constantly and get inspired. I read this book and remind myself of the person that I want to become and strive for. I gave away my power to situations in the past and now I had to start fighting for myself. I chose to fight for my

The Commandments of Womanhood

happiness and better tomorrow. I look at the younger generation of women, myself included, and I just want us to be better. We are so broken and hurt more than people will ever know. I want us to love ourselves and find joy again. I want us to celebrate the pure essence of our womanhood.

I hope you found healing and gained enlightenment within these pages as I did during while discovering The Commandments of Womanhood. Know your worth and never settle for less than you deserve. If my story and testimony can at least touch one person, I am okay with that because the more I wrote these pages I realized the glory was less about me overcoming hardships and more about God's grace over my life. People were so excited to hear that I was writing a book, and I often wondered if they would still feel that way if they saw my scars and knew my real story. When people see me, they see a strong woman; but I often wondered if they would feel the same if they knew how broken and damaged I was. The more I restored my relationship with God, the more those worries began to become irrelevant.

The Commandments of Womanhood

I found my relationship with my father again through this and I can only hope this brings you back into our dad's arms. No matter what you have been through or how dirty you think you are, it's never too late to come home to the kingdom. We have to claim back the power in our **Womanhood** and find healing. I thought I wrote this book in two weeks, but honestly this was God's way of flowing through me. After 8 months of being homeless, sleeping in some of the worst conditions of my life, I was able to find my way back home.

The Commandments of Womanhood

Stay Connected With

Emiko Love

Instagram:@thedreamgenie

Facebook:@emikothedreamgenie & @thecommandmentsofwomanhood

Blog:Mindfulblisss.blogspot.com

Made in the USA
Monee, IL
21 September 2020